Early Saints of God

BOB HARTMAN

ILLUSTRATED BY
DOUG OUDEKERK

Augsburg
MINNEAPOLIS

Family Read-Aloud Collection
Foreword by Walter Wangerin, Jr.

VOL. I

Cover design by Craig P. Claeys
Text design by Lois Stanfield, LightSource Images

_____

Library of Congress Cataloging-in-Publication Data

ISBN 0-8066-3609-2

_____

_____

Manufactured in Singapore   AF 9-3609

02   01   00   99   98   1   2   3   4   5   6   7   8   9   10

Contents

FOREWORD

Worlds to Share

WALTER WANGERIN, JR.

 ow often I wished I could companion my children through their most difficult experiences—or through their every joy. Too often I learned of the twists of their personal journeys after the fact. I hadn't been there. Moreover, if I had been, I may have been denied full access to—a full understanding of—their hearts and minds in the event.

But there is a way, a blessed way, into the hearts and minds of our children as they journey through life. When the parent reads out loud to the child, the older one becomes the younger one's most intimate companion. They travel together through dangers and delights, through adventures and mysteries, through stories, through genuine experiences—through life itself.

The power of a story well told is to create whole experiences for the child, but controlled experiences with beginnings and middles, and with good endings.

The reward for parents who read such stories to their children is an intimacy that is emotional, spiritual, and real. The walls come down; nothing is hidden between them.

And the benefits to children are legion:

- They are assured that, whatever the experience, they are not alone.

- They are fearless before the circumstances of the story, however frightening or thrilling. And, in consequence, they are prepared to meet similar circumstances in their real life with the boldness and trust that come of experience.

- They, when they laugh heartily, are empowered! For the laughter of children in the face of giants or troubles or evils is their sense of superiority. Their ability to see silliness in danger is their freedom to take spiritual steps above the danger.

- And they are granted a genuine independence, a freedom of choice. For children can choose to hear a fantasy tale as fantasy only, something fun and funny, but not anything you would meet in the real world. And they can listen to stories of distant heroes and heroic deeds as ancient history and nothing to do with their life. Or else they can choose to identify completely with the main character—in which case this fantasy or this ancient story stands for things absolutely real in their own world. Children don't make such choices consciously; they make them in the deep parts of their souls, when they are ready to take the real ride of the story. And the fact that they can and do choose grants them true personhood.

And you, their parent, are there, companioning your child through wonders and terrors, through friendships and wisdom, through experience into experience.

When my father bought a thick book containing all the tales of Hans Christian Andersen and read them to us, he did me a kindness more profound than mere entertainment. He began to weave a world that genuinely acknowledged all the monsters in mine, as well as all the ridiculous situations and silly asides that I as a child found significant. Dad/Andersen was my whispering, laughing, wise companion when I most needed companionship.

Night after night my dad would read a story in his articulate, baritone voice. Gently the voice invited me. Slowly I accepted the invitation and delivered myself to a wonderful world. And as I looked around, I discovered that this world was confident with solutions, and I was a citizen of some authority and reputation. I was no longer alone, no longer helpless.

Dad would sit in a chair beside my bed, one lamp low at his shoulder, his pipe clamped between his teeth and sending the smell of his presence and his affections to me where I lay. Mostly the room, an attic with slanted ceilings, was in darkness. The wind whistled in the eaves.

"Ready?" Dad would say.

We would nod. We would curl tight beneath the covers.

"Once upon a time," Dad would read, sending me straight through the attic walls into the night, onto the wind, for gorgeous, breathtaking flights.

What part of my being could not find affirmation in such an event? My body was present, delighting in its vicarious adventures. All my senses were alert and active, sight and sound and smell and touch. My emotions were given every opportunity—highs so tremendously high, and lows acceptable because Dad was the leader. My mind, my intellect, labored at solutions before the story itself declared them.

And all my affections were granted lovely objects. I could love in that event when my father read to us: I could love characters in the tale; I could love their qualities, their deeds, their struggles; I could love the tale itself—but mostly, I could love my father, whose very voice was his offering of love to me. We were one in this event, one in the reading and in the listening and in the experiencing.

Night after night my father read to us from that thick book. Night after night I lived the adventures that gave order to my turbulent child's experience. The tales gave shape to my waking self, to my instincts, to my faith in God, and to my adulthood yet to come. For I am what I am now, in part, because once I experienced important events within the protected sphere of my father's dear influence.

These events were deep and primal.

But on the page they were merely stories—until my father opened his mouth and read them to me.

The Saint of Christmas

SAINT NICHOLAS OF MYRA
FOURTH CENTURY

 *hen it comes right down to it, we don't actually know much about Saint Nicholas. We know he lived during the fourth century in Myra (MY-ruh), a city in what is now Turkey. We know that he was a bishop, responsible for all the churches in Myra and probably in the area around the city as well. But beyond that, most of what we know about him comes from legends told over and over again in the centuries following his death. Those tales paint the picture of a generous, kind-hearted man who had a special love for children and who was willing to sacrifice his own wealth for their good. Sound familiar? That's because the Saint Nicholas stories eventually formed the basis for another set of stories about a jolly man who gave gifts to children. In fact, if you say his name fast enough, you can almost hear the similarity: Saint Nicholas . . . Saint Nick-lus . . . Say-ni-klus . . . Santa Claus!*

I've chosen to tell one of the most famous stories about Nicholas. But because it's mostly legendary, anyway, I've taken a few liberties. I've set it back in the time when Nicholas was a simple parish priest. And I've tossed in a few "Santa Claus" references just for fun. See how many of them you can spot!

"I'VE GOT IT!" shouted Rufus. "I've got it!" And he threw his cousin's doll into the air.

"Give it back!" cried Priscilla. But Rufus just laughed and stuck out his tongue. Then he held the doll high over his head so she couldn't reach it. When she tried to jump for it, he tossed it to his brother, Timothy.

"Betcha can't catch us!" Timothy called. Then he and Rufus took off down the narrow street.

Priscilla ran after them, tears flying out the corners of her eyes. But Rufus and Timothy were too fast for her. They would have gotten clean away if they hadn't turned a corner and run straight into the belly of the local priest!

Fortunately, it was a big belly. And a soft belly. And even more fortunately, Father Nicholas was much too kind to mind.

"Ho, ho, ho!" he chuckled. "What have we here? And where are you boys off to in such a hurry?"

"N-nowhere, Father Nicholas," stammered Rufus.

And that's when the priest spotted the toy in Timothy's hand.

"So tell me, Timothy," he chuckled again. "When did you start playing with dolls?"

The boy's face flushed red with embarrassment, and then even redder with shame, when Priscilla came crying around the corner.

"I think I see what's going on, now," said Father Nicholas without a trace of humor in his voice. And he gently took the doll from Timothy.

"It was just a joke, Father," Rufus muttered. "We were gonna give it back."

"But even jokes can hurt," sighed Father Nicholas. Then he handed the doll to Priscilla and wiped her face dry with his sleeve.

"Now go and play nicely," he smiled. "And I don't want to see you boys being cruel to your cousin again."

"No, Father," said Rufus.

"Whatever you say, Father," agreed Timothy.

One week later, Father Nicholas was walking through the neighborhood again. He prayed for the sick, gave money to the poor, and stopped to listen to anyone who had a problem, a question, or a complaint. And if someone had a funny story to tell, they would always make a point of telling Father Nicholas first—just to watch his enormous belly shudder and shake!

The people loved Father Nicholas. And he loved them. Perhaps that is why he was so upset when he passed little Priscilla's house and heard her crying once again.

And unfortunately for Timothy and Rufus, that was the very same moment they chose to go racing down Priscilla's street.

"You! Boys! Stop!" Father Nicholas shouted.

"Gee, Father," Timothy complained, "it's like you're everywhere! Do you watch us all the time?"

"No," said the priest thoughtfully, "but God does. And if he's seen you teasing your little cousin again, I can guarantee that he will be very disappointed with you."

"We haven't been teasing her," said Rufus.

"Honest, Father," added Timothy.

"Then why was she crying as I passed her house?" the priest asked.

"Didn't you hear?" said Timothy. "Her father—our Uncle Crispus—lost all his money. Mom said it was in business."

"Anyway," Rufus interrupted, "Mom says he has to sell Priscilla and her two sisters as slaves so the rest of the family can have enough to live."

Father Nicholas shook his head sadly. "We must do something about this," he muttered. Then for a few moments more he said nothing at all. He just stood there stroking his long beard and thinking. Finally, he spoke.

"Boys," he said, "I'm going to need your help. Can I count on you?"

"Yes, Father," answered Rufus.

"Sure," Timothy agreed.

"Then meet me at the church tonight, just after dark. If your mother has any questions, just tell her you're with me. Your uncle is a proud man, and if I can help it, I don't want him to find out what we're doing."

"What *are* we going to do?" asked Timothy.

Father Nicholas laid a finger to the side of his nose and grinned. "You'll find out soon enough!" he said, his eyes twinkling. And off he went, leaving the boys to wonder and wait.

Before he became a priest, Nicholas had been a wealthy man. That was no longer the case, for he had given most of his money away. But Nicholas calculated that he had just enough left to save Priscilla and her sisters. He split the last of his money into three parts, poured the gold coins into three small leather bags, then tied the bags shut with leather straps. They looked just like three little presents. Then he went to the church and waited for the boys.

As promised, they came just after dark, excited by the thought of this secret mission. It was a cold night, so they had their cloaks wrapped around them and their hoods draped over their heads.

"It's awfully foggy tonight," said Rufus.

"We could hardly find our way here," added Timothy.

"Not to worry," Father Nicholas said. And he called for one of his deacons.

"Brother Rudolfus," he said, "the boys tell me it's foggy tonight, and we have to go out on an important, secret mission. Could you lend us your little oil lamp?"

"A secret mission?" grinned old Rudolfus. "Well, I'll do better than that. If you like, I'll lead you there myself."

Father Nicholas patted his deacon on the back and whispered

their destination into this ear. Then he wrapped himself up in his cloak, pulled the hood over his head, and slipped the three little bags into his pocket.

And off they went through the fog and night—the enormous priest, the two little boys, and old Rudolfus lighting the way.

When they reached Priscilla's house, Father Nicholas turned to the boys and whispered, "Now here's where you lend a hand, boys." And he pulled the bags out of his pocket and gave then to Rufus and Timothy.

"What is it?" asked Rufus.

"It's heavy," said Timothy.

"It's money!" Father Nicholas explained. "And plenty of it—or at least enough to keep your cousins from being sold into slavery. I want you to climb the garden wall and sneak it into the house."

"But how?" asked Rufus.

"I know!" suggested Timothy. "We could go up on the roof!"

"Don't be stupid!" argued Rufus. "You'd need some kind of hole to drop it through."

"How about an open window?" suggested Father Nicholas. "Just toss it in. But be careful not to hit anyone. The important thing is that it's all done in secret—that no one sees you!"

"Okay!" said the boys together. Then they scampered up over the wall.

It took forever for the boys to return—or so it felt to Father Nicholas. But when they appeared at last over the top of the wall, there was no time to lose.

"Run!" cried Timothy. "Uncle Crispus is coming!"

So off they dashed down the street, disappearing into the night.

"Stop!" called Crispus. But when he looked over the wall, all he could see were the backs of three shadowy figures—one big one, two little ones, and a dim light cutting the fog before them.

First thing the next morning, Father Nicholas went looking for his two little helpers. But before he found them, he had already heard the good news on the street.

"Did you hear, Father?" asked one woman from his church. "The night before Crispus was to sell his daughters into slavery, someone dropped three bags of gold through his window!"

"Mom says it's a miracle!" explained Rufus later.

"Uncle Crispus says it was angels!" laughed Timothy.

"The important thing is that your cousins are safe," the priest smiled. "And that stays our little secret. All right?"

"Sure," said Rufus.

"Whatever you say," agreed Timothy.

The priest winked as he thanked the boys. Then he laughed for joy—"Ho! Ho! Ho!"—until his big belly shook.

*S*lavery. This is an evil most of us know little about—thank goodness. But the sad fact is that slavery was a way of life in the ancient Roman Empire. People were bought and sold regularly, often in order to pay off debts. Yes, some slaves were treated well. But many more were abused. And, in any case, to be owned by someone else, to lose control over where you went or what you did, surely resulted in hopelessness, even in the best of situations.

And so it was not merely an amusing Christmas-morning trinket that Nicholas and his helpers dropped through the window that night. No, Saint Nicholas' gift meant the difference between slavery and freedom for those girls—maybe even the difference between death and life.

The story may be legendary, but I suspect it endured because it reflects the hopes of millions who had no one to pay for their freedom, and the gratitude of those who did.

Talk about It

- Many legends about St. Nicholas indicate that he had a special love for children. When he saw them hurting, he felt it deeply and had to do something to help. What kinds of people do you have a "special love" for? Why do you think these people are so special to you? What kinds of hurt make *you* hurt inside and make you want to help?

- In the New Testament book of Matthew (chapter 6:1–4) Jesus talks about how we should do good things for others. He says it is better to be charitable "in secret" than to let everybody know. Why do you think he says that? And what difference does giving in secret make to the person who gives, *and* to the person who receives?

Prayer

Dear God,
Help us be sensitive to the feelings of others. When we play or when we're at work or when we're just home together, help us not to say or do things—even in fun—that might cause pain. Give us compassionate hearts, hearts like that of Saint Nicholas—hearts that hurt when someone else is hurting. And give us hands that reach out to help. Amen.

The Little Girl Who Could

SAINT NINO

FOURTH CENTURY

Sometimes it's tough being a kid. There are lots of things that adults won't let you do. Some of them are for your own good, obviously—like driving to the mall, or playing with the chain saw, or letting your hamster have her babies at the bottom of your sister's bed. But sometimes adults won't let you do things because they think you're not strong enough or smart enough or big enough yet. And that's frustrating, because you'll never know if you're good at something until you try.

That's what Nino (NEE-noh) discovered. She was just a kid—a little girl who had been taken from her home, somewhere in the Roman Empire, and forced to serve as a slave up north in a land that is now part of Russia. Nobody knew about Jesus up there. Nobody had ever heard of him. And as for Nino, she wasn't a preacher or a teacher or a priest or anything. She was just a kid—a kid who followed Jesus. But when the opportunity came, Nino talked about what she knew—how Jesus loved her and had answered her prayers. And even though she didn't look big enough or strong enough or smart enough to change a nation, once they heard Nino, the people of her new land were never the same!

Everybody loved Nino. Perhaps it was her smile, or her hardworking, or her help-anyone nature.

Or maybe it was the sweet sadness she let show out the corner of her eyes when something reminded her of home.

"She's just a young girl, poor thing," the women in the village would whisper. "A little slave girl snatched away from her parents in a land far from here."

"Don't feel too sorry for her," someone would always add. "Yes, our soldiers kidnapped her. But, if they had the chance, the Romans would do the same to us."

These people had taken away Nino's freedom and her homeland and all that was familiar to her. But there was one thing they could not take away. And that was her love for Jesus and her faith in his power to help her.

One rainy morning, Nino found her mistress in tears.

"It's the baby!" her mistress wept. "He's ill. He's very ill. He's cold and he's pale and he's having trouble breathing. But nothing I do seems to make him any better!" And then she added, "In your country, is there some cure for such a thing?"

"There is," said Nino plainly. "In my home, when my brothers or my sisters or one of my parents were sick, we would ask Jesus to make them well."

"Is this Jesus a doctor, then?" Nino's mistress asked. "And would he come all the way to our country to help us?"

Nino smiled. "Jesus is better than any doctor," she said. "He is the Son of God, the creator of the world! And if you want, I will ask him to make the baby well."

Nino's mistress wiped her eyes and nodded eagerly. Nino hurried to the baby's bed. He was barely breathing now, so she wrapped him in her cloak and said a simple prayer.

"Dear Jesus," she asked, "please make this baby well, and show my mistress how good and strong you really are."

Nino handed the baby back to his mother, and they both stared hopefully at his tiny, pale face. After a little while, the color began to blush pink back into the baby's cheeks and his temperature returned to normal.

Nino's mistress started crying again. But this time the tears were a mark of her gratitude and joy. Then she ran through the village, the baby in her arms, to share that joy with her neighbors.

"Nino is just a little girl," the women whispered. "But there must be something special about her."

"And this Jesus," someone added, "he must be a very powerful god indeed!"

Word of the healing spread—from Nino's village to the next and to the next one after that. Soon it came to the attention of the queen of Nino's new land.

The queen had been ill for many years, and none of her doctors was able to cure her. So she called for her driver and her servants and her guards, and they climbed into their chariots and went to visit Nino.

Nino's mistress was shocked when the queen came knocking at her door. But she was no more shocked than the queen herself when she laid eyes on Nino.

"You really are just a little girl!" the queen exclaimed. "Tell me: how do you manage to do such extraordinary things?"

Nino smiled. "I don't do anything," she explained. "I pray to Jesus. I ask for his help. And because he is God's Son, the creator of the world, he is able to make sick people well."

"Then would you talk to him for me?" asked the queen in a humble voice, as she fell on her knees before the little girl. "I have been ill for so long. All I want, in the whole world, is to be better."

So Nino laid her little hand on the queen's head and prayed.

"Dear Jesus," she asked, "please make the queen well. Show her how good and how strong you really are."

The queen rose and thanked Nino. Then she started off for home. And mile by bumpy mile, she began to feel better and better and better.

By the time she returned, she was no longer ill at all!

"Did you hear about the queen?" the noblewomen whispered. "A little girl made her well!"

"A little girl," someone added, "and somebody called Jesus."

Several months later, the king was out in the forest hunting. It had been a good day, but as he headed for home, a thick fog fell on the woods, and he could hardly see the horse's head in front of him.

Branches snapped and cracked, beasts snarled and howled as nighttime approached. The king grew more and more frightened.

It was then that he remembered—his wife's illness, the little girl who had prayed for her, and Jesus to whom she had prayed.

And so the king shut his eyes and prayed, too. A simple prayer. A desperate prayer.

"Dear Jesus," he asked "the fog is thick, and I'm lost in the midst of it. If you will lead me safely home, I will trust you and follow you, just like the little slave girl."

The king finished his prayer. He opened his eyes. And he could not believe what he saw. The fog had lifted as quickly as it had come! He raced straight home rejoicing.

"We must send for the little slave girl!" he told the queen. "She knows more about this Jesus than anyone!"

So Nino came to live with the king and the queen. And it wasn't long before she was teaching them all about Jesus—how he died and was buried and rose from the dead.

The king and queen believed what Nino taught them, and soon she was teaching people all across the land.

"What a dear little girl!" the people said. "And what an amazing story she tells—a God who sent his Son to die for us!"

So everybody loved Nino even more. And because of her simple faith and her sad, sweet smile, they came to love Jesus, too.

*W*hat is the purpose of a sign? It points to something, doesn't it?

"Here is a McDonald's!"

"There is Main Street."

"Follow the arrows to the picnic ground."

In his account of the life of Jesus, the apostle John refers to Jesus' miracles as "signs." Why? Because they pointed to something—to the power of God at work in Jesus.

"Look! The stormy sea is calm. The God of creation is at work here."

"Look! The blind man can see. The God of light has conquered the darkness."

"Look! Lazarus is alive! The God of life has overcome death."

The miracles of healing that God performed in response to Nino's prayers were signs as well. Signs that grabbed the attention of the people who had made her a slave. Signs that gave Nino the opportunity to speak about her faith in Jesus. Signs that pointed the way to God.

Talk about It

- If you had to talk with someone who had never heard about Jesus, what are the three most important things you would tell that person about him?

- The story of why you believe in or follow Jesus is sometimes called your "testimony." Just like in a court of law, "testimony" means telling what happened. That's what Nino did. It wasn't fancy. It was just the plain simple truth. It might be interesting to talk about your own "testimony" with your family. Simply tell the story of how you came to follow Jesus and what he has done in your life. Then, if anyone should ever ask, you will be ready—just like Nino was—to tell the truth, the whole truth, and nothing but the truth!

Prayer

Dear God,

You have called us all to serve you—whether we are strong or weak, rich or poor, big or little, young or old. In those times when we are afraid because of the job you have given us, or feel inadequate to do the job well, remind us of Nino. And then help us just to do the best we can, and to leave the results up to you. Amen.

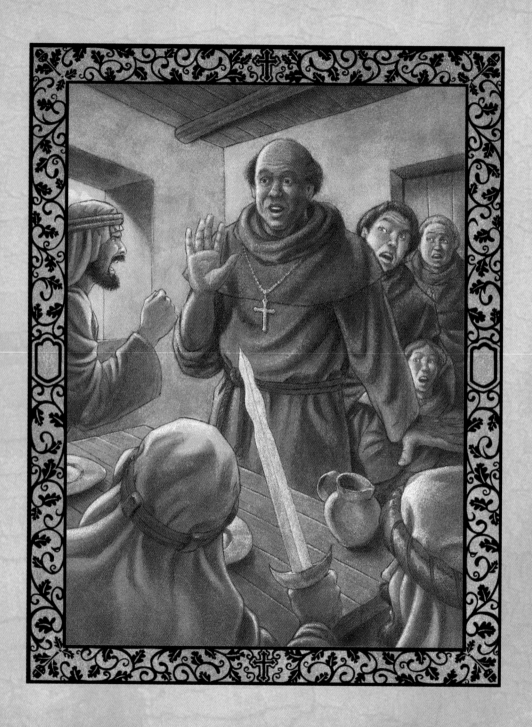

The Bandit and the Monk

SAINT MOSES THE ETHIOPIAN
A.D. 330–405

*W*here do you go to find God? In the fourth and fifth centuries, everybody knew the answer to that question. You go to the desert!

It may seem strange to us, but for over a hundred years, thousands of men and women left their homes in Rome or Damascus or Alexandria and went to live in the Egyptian desert. In those days, people believed that the desert (or any wilderness place, for that matter) was where the power of evil was strongest, and that if they could beat the devil on his own turf—with God's help, of course—they could beat him anywhere!

And so off to the desert they went. Some lived all by themselves. Others gathered in places called monasteries, which were led by a special monk called an abbot. They worked at simple jobs, refrained from pleasure, meditated on the scriptures, and spent lots of time in prayer—all in an attempt to draw closer to God.

Many of them succeeded, and their lives became such shining examples of goodness and holiness and love that their stories were written down and passed on from generation to generation. One of the most famous of these Desert Fathers (as they came to be called) was Moses the Ethiopian.

THE BOY POUNDED FRANTICALLY on the monastery door.

"They're coming! They're coming!" he shouted. "Robbers and bandits headed this way! Please let me in!"

The door cracked open, and two sleepy monks grabbed the boy and bundled him off to the abbot who led their small group. They did not hear the thundering hoofbeats that hammered along the horizon or see the clouds of dust that veiled the rising sun. But if they had, they would been every bit as frightened as the boy.

"They raided our village," the boy sobbed. "They took our money and our animals and our food…" And here he threw himself into the abbot's arms. "And they killed my father and my big brothers."

The abbot squeezed the boy tight and felt hot tears soak right through his rough brown robe.

"And what makes you think they're coming here?" the abbot asked gently.

"My mother and I were hiding. We heard them talking. And the big one—the scariest one of all—he said so. He said they were coming here next. So as soon as the sun went down, Mother sent me to warn you. I've been running all night."

The abbot squeezed the boy even more tightly. "Thank you," he whispered. But before he could say anything else, the door burst open and five fierce bearded men rushed into the room!

They were dressed all in black, and their swords were drawn, ready for battle.

The boy screamed and ran, cowering, into a corner. But the abbot did not move and did not raise his voice at all.

"You can put those away," he said quietly. "There is no one here who will fight you."

"What?" roared a voice from behind the five thieves. "Do you mean to tell me that monks are not afraid to die?"

The man who belonged to the voice pushed through the others and stood before the abbot. He was taller than them by a foot at least. Broader and stronger, too. A great lion of a man, with a face as black as his robe. "Monks fear the pain of death, certainly," said the abbot calmly. "But death itself? No. For we know that death is but the path to the home our Savior has prepared for us."

"Pretty words," the robber grunted. "So I suppose that means my friends and I are here to help you on your way!"

The thieves laughed and poked each other.

"Do what you want with us," the abbot said, "but let the child go. He can do you no harm."

At that, the big man's face grew angry. "I'll do as I please!" he bellowed. "Exactly as I please! I am Moses. Moses the Ethiopian. And no man will ever tell me what to do again!"

The abbot looked past the anger. Past the swords. Past the possibility of his own death. And right into Moses' eyes.

"Moses the Ethiopian," he said slowly. "Yes, I've heard of you. Many times, in fact. Moses the thief. Moses the murderer. Moses the violent and dangerous man. And before then: Moses . . . the slave."

"And what of it?" the robber snarled, caught now in the abbot's gaze. "Only this," the abbot smiled. "I know how to set you free. Once you were a slave to another man's will. Now you are a slave to your violence, your passion, and your greed. But God made you to be free—free to live and free to love."

Moses had battled strong men, beaten superior forces, and battered down the walls of fortified towns. But he had never faced anything as powerful as the peaceful look and the quiet voice of this old monk.

"Free?" he whispered, so that only the two of them could hear. "How? Tell me how."

"Tell God you're sorry for the wrong things you've done," the abbot whispered back. "Then ask him to forgive you. That's what Jesus died for. If he could forgive a thief while he hung on the cross, he can certainly do the same for you."

"And then what?" Moses asked.

"Live your life as God intended," the abbot said, "not for yourself but for the love of others." Then the old man smiled. "You could stay here, with us, if you like!"

And that's when the tears—an oasis of tears—rolled down the face of Moses, the desert thief.

"Leave us!" he shouted to his men. "Wait outside. There's been a change of plans."

Twenty years passed. And another boy, in another part of the desert, pounded frantically on a monastery door.

"They're coming!" he shouted. "They're coming! Robbers and bandits, headed this way!"

Two monks pulled the boy to safety. But he wasn't safe for long. The bandits burst into the courtyard and then into the abbot's quarters, where the monks and boy had run to hide.

Three monks were on their knees praying for God's protection. And the boy was huddled among them.

"Get up!" the robbers demanded. "We want your food. We want your animals. And we'll take that boy for our slave. Surrender him now, or die!"

The monks' heads remained bowed. But out from their midst came a voice. A voice as deep as a desert well.

"You may have our food," the voice said slowly. "And you may have our animals." Here the voice grew firm and sure. "But no one is going to be your slave."

And with that, the abbot stood to face the bandits. He was taller than any of them by a foot at least. Broader and stronger, too. A great lion of a man—and his face was as black as a desert night.

The thieves dropped back and reached for their swords. This was the biggest man they had ever seen. And he had the look of one who feared nothing, not even death.

He spoke calmly and quietly. "My brothers will be leaving now," he said. "And they will take the boy with them. In exchange, you can do whatever you like with me."

Then he nodded, and off they went—the monks and the boy—out the back of the monastery and into the desert.

And that's when one of the bandits spoke.

"I know you," he said. "Or at least I know of you. You are Moses. Moses the Ethiopian. You were once a thief like us."

"Yes, I was," the abbot nodded sadly. "A murderer. A bandit. A slave to my own greed." Then he smiled. "But God changed me. He set me free, and for twenty years now I have lived in his love and for the sake of others. My life has never been better. And what is more," he added, "God can do the same for you."

"Nonsense!" shouted one of the thieves.

"Rubbish!" shouted another.

"You've stalled us long enough!" shouted a third.

And, drawing their swords, the thieves rushed at the abbot and struck him where he stood.

He made no move to stop them, to fight them, to answer their blows in any way. Instead, he thought of the monks—his brothers—and the boy who were, even now, making their escape. Then, shutting his eyes, he died.

And Moses the Ethiopian was free forevermore.

*M*oses the Ethiopian was buried in the monastery where he served—in the middle of the desert where he had lived and where he died. There are still monks living in the desert, living in that very monastery, in fact. Praying and working and serving God, just like Moses did all those years ago!

Talk about It

- The abbot pointed out that Moses was first a slave to another man and then a slave to his violence and greed. What did he mean by that? Is there some bad habit or attitude that has made a slave of you? Using Moses's life as an example, talk about ways that you can be set free from the wrong things that control you.

- Moses could have fought and maybe even beaten the bandits who killed him. But instead he chose not to defend himself, following the example of Jesus, who said that we should "turn the other cheek" to those who strike us on one cheek. Are there ever any situations in which it might be right to fight back? Talk about those situations and explore the peaceful options that might be open to you.

Prayer

Dear God,
Thank you for setting us free. Through the life of Jesus, you set us free from the power of temptation. Through the death of Jesus, you set us free from the grip of guilt. Through the resurrection of Jesus, you set us free from the hopelessness of death. Thank you for Jesus. Thank you for setting us free! Amen.

A *Good* and *Stubborn Woman*

SAINT MARCELLA
A.D. 325–410

ich. Well-connected. Incredibly intelligent. If Marcella were alive today, she might be a powerful politician; the owner of a penthouse in New York, Paris, or London; or the head of a big movie studio. In her day, she sat at the very top of Roman society. But when she heard the story of Jesus, she knew that wasn't enough. At the first opportunity, she gave away her riches, keeping only her mansion to be used as a gathering place for like-minded Roman women. A small religious community grew up there and lasted for many years.

But then everything changed. The Roman Empire, which many Romans believed would last forever, began to crumble and fall apart. Economic problems, moral problems, or just plain old apathy—there are many explanations for its collapse—but it wasn't long before foreign armies marched into Rome and destroyed everything Marcella had once treasured. Everything but her faith, that is. And that faith was something she needed more than ever when those barbarian soldiers came knocking at her door.

 THE WHIP CRACKED AND SNAPPED against the old woman's back. Five times. Ten times. Twenty times. With each blow came the same question.

"Where have you hidden your treasure?"

She had answered the first time, the second time, and the twentieth time: "There is no treasure. I have given it all away."

By now she could barely speak. Her lips were cracked and dry, her back red and raw. And, besides, her torturers did not believe her anyway. So what was the use?

At last, the beating stopped. The next thing Marcella knew, she was back in her cell, lying next to young Principia (prin-SIP-ee-uh), her student and her friend.

Marcella was eighty-five years old. If her parents had had their way, she would have been a grandmother by now—a great-grandmother, perhaps—and the matron of a wealthy Roman family. Instead she was a prisoner.

And Rome? Rome lay in ruins outside her window, its streets thick with the smell and strange accents of invading barbarian soldiers.

Marcella wanted to sleep. But the stinging wounds on her back made it impossible to find a comfortable position. So she lay her head on her young friend's lap and began to talk.

"I had been married only seven months when my husband died. I was young, wealthy, and well-educated, the daughter of a noble family. So my parents were determined that I should marry again and marry well.

"The Consul, Cerealis (ser-ee-AL-is)—that's who they wanted me to marry—the uncle of Caesar himself!"

Marcella shifted and groaned and then smiled.

"I was always the stubborn one," she chuckled. "That's what my parents said. And they were right. Cerealis was the perfect match for me, but I would not have him. For One I loved even more was calling me in a very different direction."

"Another man?" asked Principia innocently.

"The Son of man," Marcella said with a smile. "The Lord Jesus—that's who was calling me. So I gave up any thoughts of marriage and promised to serve him and him alone in any way I could."

"But what about your parents?" asked Principia. "What did they do?"

"There wasn't much they *could* do," Marcella said. "I had inherited my husband's treasure, remember? I was wealthy. So I could do as I pleased. And the first thing I did was to give that treasure away—to the poor, to the sick, to anyone who needed it. Nothing has ever brought me more joy!"

The old woman shut her eyes for a moment, and Principia thought she was finally falling asleep. But a sudden scream from somewhere down the hall woke her with a start.

"Where was I?" Marcella asked.

"You were giving your money away," Principia reminded her.

"Yes, yes. But I still had my house—the big place up on the Aventine (AH-vun-teen) Hill. I spent my days reading and praying and caring for any who needed my help. And soon other women came to join me. Some were rich and well educated like myself. Others were quite poor. It didn't matter, really. What mattered was the company—the fact that we were together. And that we were serving Jesus.

"We carried on quite happily for many years. And then, of course, Jerome came along."

"Jerome?" asked Principia, curiously. "You don't mean *the* Jerome?"

"The very one!" Marcella grinned. "Scholar. Teacher. Writer. And now I hear he's translated the whole of the scriptures into

Latin. He's the most famous Christian in the world, I suppose. And probably the most brilliant. But . . ."

"But?" asked Principia.

"But, like most men," Marcella finished, "he likes to be in charge."

"Was he in charge of you?" Principia asked.

"Not at first. Our little group of women admired him, of course. And some of us even began to help him with his research and writing."

"Really?" gasped Principia.

"Oh, yes!" Marcella assured her. "What do they say? Behind every great man there is a woman. Well, there were many women behind Jerome. Remember, some of us were educated in the very best schools in Rome. Unfortunately, Jerome did not always appreciate that. If you'd read his writings, you'd know—he can be very arrogant and rude—brutal even—when he tries to argue his point."

"So you gave in to him, then," Principia asked, "when there was a disagreement?"

"No!" Marcella answered, her chin set firm. "Not if I was right. Not if the life of our little community was at stake. No, I stood up to him. And as a result, we developed a very deep and healthy respect for one another. Some might even call it a kind of love."

"So you were in love with him?" Principia gasped again.

"No. Of course not." Marcella sighed. "He was seventeen years my junior, for a start. And I had taken a vow to serve the Lord, remember? But we did come to appreciate each other's mind; each other's strength; and, I suppose, each other's stubbornness! And through it all, we did a lot of good. Maybe there's a lesson in there somewhere: if God can use an arrogant genius like Jerome and a hardheaded old woman like me, he can probably use anybody!"

Principia smiled. "So what happened to him?" she asked.

"He moved to Bethlehem," said Marcella softly. "Jerome could never stay in one place for very long. Several of the women went with him. He wanted me to go as well. But I believed that my place was here in Rome. It was stubbornness that drew us together and, in the end, I suppose it was stubbornness that tore us apart."

Just then the clanking of swords and shields and the thudding of soldiers' footsteps announced the return of Marcella's torturers.

"The captain wants to talk to her again," grunted one of the voices.

"With a house that big, there's bound to be treasure somewhere," grunted the other.

But Marcella and Principia could not understand the foreign words these barbarians spoke.

"If they take me," Marcella whispered, "I will not survive another beating. There is a little—a very little—bit of money left in the house. It's hidden in the wall in the far corner of the main room. Behind the statue. You know the place. Make sure it gets to the poor."

"But you must tell them where it is," Principia pleaded. "Perhaps then they will let you go."

"They would only want more," Marcella sighed. "And that really is all that is left. Besides, I promised I would give it away. And I shall. I'm stubborn, remember?" Marcella grinned. "Good and stubborn."

"Stubborn. And good," said Principia, fighting back her tears as the soldiers burst into the room and dragged her old friend away.

Marcella survived that last beating. And when the soldiers returned to torture Principia, Marcella's tears convinced them to leave the young woman alone. In fact, they were so moved (by her courage and stubbornness, perhaps?), that they transferred both Marcella and Principia to a local church.

In that church a few days later, the old woman died of her wounds, cradled in the arms of her friend.

When we think of saints, we sometimes conjure up pictures of gentle, kind, and meek individuals. And some saints fit that picture. But many, like Marcella and Jerome, weren't like that at all. They had their faults just like the rest of us, and God used them in spite of those faults. In fact, it's possible that those faults are often just a dark reflection of what makes us useful to God in the first place.

Jerome, for example, was one of the greatest thinkers of his day. He wrote volume after volume defending the church's teaching and explaining the Bible. He studied in Rome, meditated in the desert, served under a pope, and translated the whole Bible into Latin. But the same determination and perfectionism that helped him accomplish so much were also the cause of his impatience, his quick temper, and the sometimes cruel attacks he leveled at those who disagreed with him.

This is not to excuse Jerome's faults, but only to suggest that all of us—even the best of us—are only "on the way" to being what God wants us to be. And if God had to wait until we were perfect to use us, we would never be of use. Like Marcella and Jerome, we need to let God work through us whenever and wherever he can, and then trust in God's mercy to make up for whatever goodness or love we lack.

Talk about It

- If you had enough money to buy anything you wanted, what are the first three things you would buy? How hard do you think it would be, then, to have to give those things away—along with the rest of your money? If you had to go from being very rich to being very poor, what would your biggest worries be?

- Things don't always work out the way our parents plan them. Marcella's parents hoped she would marry Caesar's uncle, but both God and Marcella had something different in mind. Talk with your parents or your grandparents. What did *their* parents want them to be? Did things turn out that way? Why? And did God have anything to do with it?

Prayer

Dear God,
You have asked us to follow Jesus. You have challenged us to live like he did. Help us to follow the example of his life. And when we fail, thank you for the forgiveness that comes to us through his death. Amen.

The Fire of Easter

SAINT PATRICK

A.D. 385–461

*I*f anyone ever had a reason to hate the Irish, it was Patrick. It's strange, isn't it, that the one man whose name has come to be identified with that nation was not, in fact, Irish at all!

Patrick was a Briton, born on the west coast of what we now call Wales, in one of the remote corners of the Roman Empire. His father was a local official who ran his own estate, and it is likely that Patrick (or Patricius—pat-REE-shus—as he was probably called) received the kind of cultured middle-class upbringing that was available across the empire. Unfortunately, in Patrick's time the empire was falling apart, and the Pax Romana—the "peace" enforced by Roman rule—was no longer a guarantee of protection against foreign invaders. So when a band of Irish pirates landed on the shores near Patrick's home, they had little trouble abducting him and carrying him off to Ireland to be sold as a slave.

For six long years, Patrick, the Roman boy, tended sheep and cattle for his Irish master. And the isolation, loneliness, and abuse could quite easily have turned into hatred—hatred for his master and hatred for his master's race. But something happened on those lonely Irish hills, something that changed Patrick, and all of Ireland, and some say, even the world!

THERE ARE SOME THINGS a man never forgets. Sights and sounds. Smells, particularly. And suffering. Maybe suffering most of all.

Patrick stood at the top of Slane Hill, watching the sun drag its orange face below the western mountains into the western sea. And, for a moment, Patrick's head was full of things he could not forget.

There were sights—the Irish hills and woods. And, yes, that same setting Irish sun.

There were sounds—Irish farmers calling their cattle in that strange, dancing Irish tongue.

There were smells—burning peat, sheep droppings, grass so green and sweet you could almost swallow its springtime perfume.

But most of all there was hurt—for Patrick was just a boy when he first came in contact with those sights and sounds and smells. A sixteen year old, kidnapped by Irish pirates, taken from his home in Britain, and sold as a slave to an Irish king.

Each night for six long years, he had stood on the top of a hill much like this one, hating what had happened to him, desperate to be free.

Now, thirty years later, Patrick watched as darkness swallowed up the Irish hills.

"Dark" is how Patrick remembered his early days in Ireland.

There was nothing but fear at first. Fear of the pirates—their bushy beards and painted faces. Fear of a language he could not understand. Fear of new places and strange ways, and fear of his master, Milcho.

Then fear turned into something else—into loneliness and resentment. Would he ever see his parents again? His home? Why had this happened to him?

His friends were all at school, studying their lessons, learning to become good Britons. Patrick might have been with them, fast on his way to becoming a lawyer or a teacher or a civil servant like his father. But instead he was stuck in this faraway place tending cattle and sheep and pigs. Tired and hungry and alone.

Patrick remembered. Patrick remembered well. For it was the loneliness that finally turned his fear and resentment in one more direction.

Far from home, without family or friends, Patrick had begun to pray.

He'd prayed before, of course. His parents were Christians. His father was a deacon in the church, in fact. But there was never much heart in their religion. Christianity was the Roman emperor's faith, and good civil servants just went along.

These hilltop prayers were different. They were desperate, anguished prayers. Real prayers. And through them Patrick grew close to God, and came to follow his Son, Jesus, who died and was buried and who rose again on Easter morning.

Easter morning! Patrick stood at the top of Slane Hill and grinned. The setting sun. The dark of night. Easter morning was just a few hours away now. It was time—time to let go of his memories and, as was the custom of his time, it was time to light the Easter fire.

Patrick knew, however, that on a hilltop not far away, Laoghaire (LEER-ee), high king of all Ireland, was about to light a fire of his own. For tonight was also Beltane (BELL-tain), a pagan feast that marked the end of winter and the beginning of spring.

The druid (DROO-id) priests gathered round King Laoghaire, chanting praises to spirits of water and stone and trees, their hands red with the blood of human sacrifice. They knew exactly what was supposed to happen on this night of Beltane. The high king would light his fire and then, in response, fires would be lit on every hill in the land. And woe to anyone who lit his fire first.

King Laoghaire held his torch at the ready and gazed out upon his land. All Ireland was bathed in darkness. The time had come. But before he could set the torch to the pile of branches and logs, another fire—Patrick's Easter fire!—sprang to life on a hilltop not far away!

"What is the meaning of this?" he cried to his priests. "Who dares usurp my right to light the first fire?"

The priests looked at one another, trembling and amazed.

"I do not know, Your Majesty," said one of them at last. "But I can promise you this: if that fire is not put out immediately, its light will spread across this land and burn in Ireland forever!"

The king called for eight of his chariots. And along with the priests and a company of his strongest armed men, he followed that light to Slane Hill.

Patrick heard them coming. He remembered well the sound of horses' hooves and chariot wheels and the battle cries of Irish warrior kings. But, this time, Patrick was not afraid.

The huge bonfire blazing behind him, Patrick started down the side of Slane Hill. And each step reminded him of the path that had brought him back to this place:

His escape from Ireland after six years of slavery.

His long years of study to become a priest.

His ordination as a bishop in the church.

His return, at last, to his home in Britain.

And, finally, his dream—the Irish places, the Irish faces, the Irish voices crying to him: "Holy boy, come and walk among us again."

That dream had become Patrick's dream, and tonight that dream would come true. He had returned to Ireland. Tonight he would preach God's freedom to the very people who had enslaved him. How good it would be to bring this good news to his former enemies, to forgive the hurts of long ago.

Patrick reached the bottom of the hill, and the high king was there to meet him. His warriors were at his side, their beards bushy, their faces painted, just like the pirates' had been.

But Patrick was no longer a boy. And Patrick was no longer afraid.

He raised his arms to the sky, and the fire of Easter sent his shadow towering high over the king and all his men.

"Some put their trust in chariots and some in horses," Patrick proclaimed, "but we will walk in the name of the Lord our God."

The druids shouted, and the armed men shouted with them: "Death to the man who dares disturb our feast!"

But Laoghaire the high king was silent. Perhaps it was Patrick's courage. Maybe it was the conviction in his voice. Or perhaps it was the fact that the king's own gods had not struck this unbeliever down or extinguished his hilltop fire. Whatever the reason, the king turned his chariot around and quietly led his people away. And the following day—Easter Day—he invited Patrick to his palace to tell him about this strange new God.

And just as the druid priest had predicted, Patrick's message spread like fire across all Ireland. He lived to see the Irish people transformed by that message, bathed in the light of God's forgiveness and love. Saint Patrick's Easter Fire still burns in Ireland, and the message of Easter truth has spread around the world!

In Patrick's time, Ireland was carved up into many local tribes, each ruled by a king. The rivalries between these kings were responsible for much violence in the land. As Christianity spread, Patrick wisely appointed bishops to serve alongside these local kings, both to care for the people's spiritual needs and to put a stop to the rulers' violence and greed. He also campaigned vigorously against the Irish slave trade. As a result of these measures, slavery was abolished and Ireland quickly became a peaceful place in which to live.

At the same time, however, the Roman Empire was being overrun by invading armies, and much of what was once the "civilized world" fell into chaos and what are called the "Dark Ages." And so it happened that the preservation of ancient culture—Greek and Roman poems and plays and essays and stories, not to mention the Holy Scriptures—fell to Ireland, the last place of peace and security in the Western world. For years thereafter, Irish monks copied and illustrated these texts with beautiful drawings and stunning colors, and kept them safe for us today. And that is why it may be argued that Patrick's willingness to forgive and to share the gospel with his former captors resulted in the salvation not only of Ireland, but of the whole Western world.

Talk about It

- Have you ever had a hard time forgiving someone who hurt you? Talk about that time—about how you felt toward that person and what finally helped you to forgive.

- Maybe there is someone you need to forgive. Or maybe you need to ask someone's forgiveness for some wrong things you have done. Ask God to help you either to seek or to offer forgiveness. Remember: forgiveness might not seem like such a big thing, but Patrick's willingness to forgive made—quite literally—all the difference in the world!

Prayer

Here is a section from a prayer often ascribed to Patrick. It is called "Saint Patrick's Breastplate" because it is a prayer of protection. These lines ask for the presence and help of Jesus in everything we do:

Christ with me, Christ before me, Christ behind me,
Christ in me, Christ beneath me, Christ above me,
Christ on my right, Christ on my left,
Christ when I lie down, Christ when I sit down,
Christ when I arise,
Christ in the heart of everyone who thinks of me,
Christ in the mouth of everyone who speaks of me,
Christ in every eye that sees me,
Christ in every ear that hears me.

Jackals, Apostles, and Palm Leaves

SAINT JOHN THE SHORT
FIFTH CENTURY

ho's your favorite athlete? A football or tennis star, maybe? An Olympic swimmer or gymnast? We often look up to athletes because, at their best, they are examples of strength and speed and discipline and endurance.

In the fifth century, nobody played football or tennis. But the people had athletes to look up to, nonetheless. They called them "The Athletes of God," but we know them as the Desert Fathers.

That's right, all those monks scratching out a living in the Egyptian desert were athletes of God. The race they ran was a race of faithfulness to God and, just like famous athletes today, they became role models—examples for others to follow.

Some were examples of bravery—like Moses the Ethiopian, whom you read about in the earlier story "The Bandit and the Monk."

Some were examples of kindness—like Theon (THAY-on), who fed and tended the desert animals.

Some were examples of forgiveness—like Gelasius (guh-LAY-see-us), who would rather show mercy to a thief than turn him in.

And some, like Saint John the Short, were examples of patience.

A LION ROARED. A jackal cried. But the little monk was not disturbed by their twilight conversation. Stooped and sandal-footed, he skittered across the desert like an old brown beetle, muttering and mumbling to keep himself company. "Must not forget. Must not forget. Must not forget."

Finally, he reached his destination, and what was left of the sunlight sent his shadow stumbling against the wall of a small stone hut.

"Abbot John," he called. "Abbot John," he croaked, "I know the hour is late, but I am badly in need of your advice."

There was silence for a moment, and then a gentle voice replied, "Come in, Brother Paul, and set yourself down."

Brother Paul crept through the doorway and, by the dim light of the oil lamp, found a seat across from Abbot John, the small, kindly man who was the monastery's leader. The abbot was slowly weaving a basket from a pile of palm leaves.

"It's my memory," Brother Paul began, "I forget where I've put things. I forget what I've said. I forget who I'm talking to, where I've been, or where I'm going. Why, it's only by God's grace that I've found my way here tonight. I know I'm an old man, but still . . ."

"Still you find it frustrating," nodded Abbot John. "Anyone would."

"Would what?" asked a suddenly puzzled Brother Paul.

"Find forgetfulness frustrating."

"Forgetfulness?" the old man repeated to himself. "Yes. Of course! Forgetfulness! That's what I've come about, isn't it? You see, I'd forgotten already!"

Abbot John smiled—an amused smile, but a kindly smile, too. "I think I can help you, but you must listen very carefully.

"First," he said, holding up one broad palm leaf, "you must repeat whatever you fear forgetting, over and over again. Let us say twelve times. Once for each of the apostles."

"Twelve times," the old man said. "Once for each apostle."

Abbot John picked up another palm leaf. "Next," he continued, "you must try to connect the name of whatever you want to remember with something familiar—something you already know. For example, if you wanted to remember my name, you might say 'John, who laughs like a jackal.' Do you see?"

"John—Jackal," the old man repeated. "Yes, I think I do!"

"And finally," suggested Abbot John as he raised a third palm leaf, "you must pray for God's help in this matter. Now, do you think you can remember these three simple instructions?"

Brother Paul squinted his eyes and twisted his face. He was thinking very hard. Then he picked up the first palm leaf.

"Twelve times—for the twelve apostles," he said.

He picked up the second leaf.

"John—Jackal," he chuckled. "Your name is John."

And finally, he picked up the third leaf.

"Pray for God's help."

"Excellent!" smiled Abbot John. Then he reached for a spare oil lamp and lit it from his own. "Now take this and find your way home. But be careful. It's very late."

"Thank you," the old man said. "Thank you very much. Your advice seems to be working already." Then he scooped up the three palm leaves and ducked out the door.

"I'll bring back the lamp tomorrow," he called. "I won't forget! Farewell, Abbot . . . Abbot . . . Jackal!"

"No, it's *John*," called the abbot. "My name is *John*."

But it was too late. Brother Paul had already wandered off into the night. And with each passing footstep, he got more and more muddled.

"Twelve jackals," he muttered. "John the Apostle. And something about the laughter of God."

The next evening, Abbot John heard a familiar rustling and shuffling outside his hut door.

"Hello," he called. "Is someone there?"

A mutter and a mumble and an embarrassed cough came tumbling out of the dusky night.

"It's me," a sad voice said. "It's Brother Paul. I am so sorry to have to bother you again, but I am afraid my forgetfulness is no better."

"Come in, then," the abbot called kindly, "and I'll see what I can do."

Brother Paul crept in, cradling an unlit lamp in one hand and clutching three crumpled palm leaves in the other.

"I tried!" he moaned. "I really did! I counted twelve jackals, and thought about the apostles, and asked God to help me remember someone named John. But my memory is as bad as ever. Help me, please!"

Abbot John smiled a sad and sympathetic smile.

"I see," he said. "Well, let me explain again." And taking the three battered palm leaves, he repeated what he had told the old man the night before. After he had finished, Brother Paul was grinning again.

"I think I have it this time," he said, taking back the palm leaves. "Twelve apostles. John—Jackal. Pray to God. See?"

"Very good!" nodded Abbot John. Then, once again, he lit the spare lamp from his own. "Now take this. And be careful."

"I will," promised Brother Paul. "And I will remember to bring it back tomorrow. You can count on it."

Then he ducked through the doorway and out into the darkness.

"Thank you, again!" he called. "Thank you, Apostle John!"

"It's *Abbot! Abbot* John," the abbot sighed. But again it was too late. As the monk wandered off into the night, darkness settled on his mind once more.

"Laugh twelve times. Apostles and jackals. Oh, dear," he muttered, "I really am a sad and useless old man."

The next day, Abbot John was not at all surprised when Brother Paul failed to return the lamp. And he was even less surprised when the falling darkness brought with it, once again, the sound of the old man's embarrassed voice.

"Forgive me," he wept. "I'm a stupid, foolish, forgetful old man who has no right to bother you night after night after night."

"Nonsense," answered Abbot John as gently as he could. And he welcomed the old man and wiped the tears from his wrinkled face.

"Now give me the palm leaves," he said, "and we'll go over it again."

"What's the use?" sighed Brother Paul. "It's just a waste of your time. You could be helping someone else. Why throw away your wisdom on an old fool like me?"

"Listen to me," said Abbot John firmly. "And listen carefully. You are not stupid or useless or foolish. And I am not wasting my time or my wisdom when I try to help you. Look at this, Brother Paul."

Abbot John took the spare lamp and lit it one more time from his own.

"Now tell me," he said "does my little lamp lose anything when it passes the flame on to yours?"

Brother Paul thought for a moment. "No," he answered. "It is as bright as ever. And now my lamp is bright, too."

"Exactly!" smiled Abbot John. "And it is just the same when I give you my help. It takes nothing away from me, no matter how many times I do it."

And that's when another light went on—inside Brother Paul!

"So you don't care how many times I come to you?" he asked.

"Not at all," said Abbot John. "For you are as precious to me as any who dwells in this desert."

Who knows what caused it? Abbot John's patience? Or his prayers? Or maybe just his willingness to give the old monk some of his time. But from that moment on, Brother Paul was no longer troubled by forgetfulness.

Palm leaves and jackals.

Apostles and abbots.

Brother Paul never confused them again. Nor did he ever again forget the name of the short, kindly man who had shared his light and his wisdom.

And the desert rang with his laughter whenever he remembered that he was not a useless old man, after all.

Short in stature, maybe, but never short of patience—that was Abbot John. Even as a young monk he showed amazing persistence. On one occasion, the monk who was responsible for training John stuck a stick in the ground. "Water that," the older monk told him as a test of John's willingness to obey. So John watered the stick—not for a day or a week or a month, but for three years—until at last it bloomed and bore fruit! In a way, that old stick was just like Brother Paul. All he needed was a little time, a little attention, and lots of patience until he could "bloom," too.

Talk about It

- Name something someone else does that really annoys you. How can you be more patient with that person? Is there a way to help that person avoid doing whatever it is that "bugs" you? Or, better, is there a way to change how you feel about that person and what bugs you?

- Does helping someone else really cost us nothing, as Abbot John suggested? Does it really take no "fire from our candles"? When we help someone else, what does it take away from our lives? And what might it add?

Prayer

Dear God,
Sometimes the people around us—even people we love—annoy us and frustrate us. Help us to be patient and treat them with kindness and gentleness and respect. Help us to change what we can, and to wait for you to change what we can't. And because none of us is perfect, help us be patient with ourselves as well. Amen.

The Woman Who Saved the City

SAINT GENEVIEVE
A.D. 420–500

*I*magine for a moment what would happen to you and your family if your country should suddenly lose its power in the world and be invaded by foreign armies.

Tanks rumbling through the malls and shopping areas. Playing fields trampled by angry troops. Movie theaters blown to pieces. Food taken from your refrigerator to feed enemy soldiers.

And, of course, there would be horrible fighting—neighbors and friends and family killed defending your town. Innocents struck by shrapnel or stray bullets.

It's a scary picture, isn't it? And awfully hard to believe. But it's just what the citizens of the Roman Empire faced when the greatest superpower the world had ever known grew weak and then fell to its enemies.

One of the fiercest of those enemies was Attila (uh-TILL-uh) the Hun. He and his armies came from what is now called Hungary and swept across the crumbling empire, killing, stealing, and destroying all along the way.

The last thing that anyone wanted to hear was "Attila is coming!" But that is exactly the message that God gave to a woman named Genevieve, who lived in Paris—not so she could predict the city's destruction, but that through her warning the city might be saved.

"ATTILA IS COMING!" warned Genevieve. "He is God's judgment on us. And he will destroy our city unless we ask God's forgiveness and pray for God's help." Everywhere she went, up and down the streets of Paris, her message was the same. But the people of Paris did not like what they heard.

"Foolish woman!"

"Prophet of Doom!"

That's what they called her, and they refused to heed her warning.

But day by day and mile by mile, the army of Attila the Hun was, indeed, marching closer and closer to Paris. And the closer the army got, the more loudly Genevieve sounded her warning.

"Attila is coming!" she cried. "We have disobeyed God, and Attila is the instrument of God's judgment. The only way we can save ourselves and our city is to fall on our knees and ask God's forgiveness."

But still the people were not convinced.

"Liar!" they shouted. "Fear monger! Keep your opinions to yourself and stop frightening our children!"

Genevieve did not know what to do. She believed her message was from God. But how could she prove it? What she needed was help, the help of someone whom the citizens of Paris respected. And so she went to visit Justus, archdeacon and assistant to her old friend Bishop Germanus (jer-MAN-us).

"They just won't believe me!" she wept. "The common people are simply frightened—they don't want to hear that such a thing could happen. And the clergy—they think this is all about power. They say I'm trying to set myself up as some sort of spokesperson for God."

"And what do you think?" asked Justus calmly.

Genevieve sighed. "I think God has given me this message and that he wants me to pass it on. It's a hard message, I'll admit—one nobody wants to hear. But does that make it any less true?"

Justus looked at the young woman before him. He looked into her piercing eyes and beyond her intense gaze. And he thought he saw what Bishop Germanus had seen all those years ago.

"I understand you were only seven when you first met the bishop," he said.

"Yes," answered Genevieve. She lowered her eyes and wandered back into her past. "We were living just outside of Paris then. I was tending a few of my father's sheep. And when the bishop passed through town, he stopped and stooped down to talk with me. And that's when we both knew.

"'I want to live my life for God,' I told him.

"The bishop smiled at me. 'And I believe he wants you to do this,' he said in return.

"From that time on, he kept his eye on me, encouraging and supporting my choice as best he could. He was there to comfort me when my parents died and I moved to Paris to live with my grandmother. And when I turned fifteen, it was the bishop himself who heard my vows of chastity and directed me to the life of prayer and service to the poor which I follow to this day."

"And the miracles . . . ?" asked Justus.

"The miracles—and the prophecies—began some time after. God used me—that's all—to heal some people and to pass his messages on to others. I'm nothing special. I'm really not. But because of the miracles, or perhaps because of the attention the bishop gave me, others have grown jealous of my work. And they have said evil things about me."

Genevieve sighed again—a sigh of sorrow and of loss. "I miss the bishop so much. He did all he could to protect me from that jealousy. But ever since he died, I have had to face it alone. And now—especially now—when the message is so important, when so much is at stake, I need that help more than ever. That's why I've come to you."

Justus stared at the ground, thinking. He'd heard the rumors and the talk—the priests complaining about this common girl who thought she could speak for God. But when he looked up again and into her eyes, he knew the choice he had to make.

"Well, I'm not the bishop," he admitted, "but I will do what I can."

They returned to the streets of Paris—Justus and Genevieve. What they found was panic and chaos and fear.

Someone grabbed them and shouted in their faces: "Attila is coming! Attila the Hun! Flee the city! Run for your lives!"

"No!" Genevieve shouted back. But before she could say one more word, the man was gone.

"You don't think they should flee?" asked Justus.

"No," Genevieve answered. "The prophecy was very clear. If we are to be saved, we must stay in the city and pray. But how will I ever convince anyone of that now?"

"Look, there is the church," said Justus. "There may yet be a way."

They pushed through the panicked crowds and fought their way to the church door.

"Ring the bell!" Justus demanded. "I am Archdeacon Justus, servant of the late Bishop Germanus, and I need to speak to the people of Paris!"

The bell began to ring, and slowly the people gathered around the church—some out of confusion, many out of fear, and many more in hope of a message that Attila was not coming after all.

"People of Paris!" Justus shouted. "I was archdeacon to Bishop Germanus, a man you knew and loved. I am here to tell you what you must do if you are to be saved. There is a woman with me whose words you need to hear."

Genevieve climbed up the church steps. But as soon as the people recognized her, they began to boo and jeer.

"False Prophet! False Prophet!" they called.

"People of Paris!" Justus shouted again, over and over until the roar died down. "People of Paris, tell me what is false about this woman. You may not like what she has told you, but her prophecy has already, in part, come true! As she foretold, Attila is marching toward this city. So you would do well to listen to her and obey all she has to say, for I believe she truly speaks for God."

Genevieve climbed the steps again. And this time there were no voices raised against her.

"My friends. My fellow citizens," she began. "It brings me no joy to share these words with you. We are in serious trouble, and it is because we have not been faithful to God.

"However, God has provided a way out! We must not run. But instead we must trust God, remain in the city, and pray for forgiveness."

Again the crowd erupted.

"Stay in the city?"

"Pray for forgiveness?"

"The woman must be mad!"

"Hear me, people of Paris!" shouted Justus for a third time. "Hear me now! This woman has been right so far. And our only salvation lies in trusting her words. If you leave the city, you may well find yourself running straight into the hands of the barbarians.

"But I know what I will do. I will stay here and pray. For I believe that God has spoken through Genevieve!

"Now go! Go to your homes and pray with us. Confess your sins. Ask God to forgive you. And trust that God will keep his word and that the city will be spared."

Slowly the crowd dispersed. Some still insisted on leaving the city. But many more did just as Genevieve told them. They went to their homes, fell on their knees, and prayed. They admitted that they had been leading sinful lives, that they had forgotten about God and God's love. Then they asked God to show mercy by forgiving them and sparing their city.

They prayed all that day and through the night—Genevieve and Justus and many of the people in Paris. And the next morning, the church bells rang again.

Yawning and rubbing their eyes, the people made their way to the church. There they found Justus on the steps.

"People of Paris!" he called. "I have just received news from one of our messengers. Early this morning, Attila came to the road that leads into Paris. He stopped there and he waited—he and his entire army. Then, for some reason—and we know that reason!—he turned south and marched away from the city. My friends, Paris is saved! And we have God and Genevieve to thank for it!"

A roar erupted from the crowd, a roar of relief and gratitude and joyous celebration. The people swarmed around Genevieve to thank her, to congratulate her, even to apologize to her. And from that moment on, she was never again known as "that foolish girl" or "that false prophet," but as "the woman who saved the city"!

*G*enevieve *helped save the city on one other occasion as well. When the Franks surrounded Paris with their armies, no one could get in or out. The enemy soldiers hoped the citizens would run out of food and surrender rather than starve. But the Franks hadn't counted on Genevieve. She was not only a prophet, but a brave and clever woman as well. She organized a secret convoy to sneak through the blockade and bring food from the countryside back to the starving Parisians. No wonder she came to be greatly revered and is now considered the patron saint of Paris.*

Talk about It

- Have you ever had an idea or an opinion you thought was good and right—or even God-pleasing, but which everyone around you thought was stupid? Talk about how that made you feel and how you dealt with it.

- Attila's nickname was "The Scourge of God," because it was widely believed throughout the Roman Empire that Attila had been sent to punish nations for their immorality and spiritual decay. That was certainly Genevieve's message—along with the hope that such punishment might lead to repentance and a return to God. It's a message that Old Testament prophets found themselves telling God's people of Israel as well. Do you think that God ever *makes* bad things happen to people today in order to draw them back to him? Are all bad things that happen some kind of message from God?

Prayer

Dear God,
For all the ways you speak to us:
> *the beauty of your creation,*
> *the words of Scripture,*
> *the presence of your Spirit,*
> *the life of your Son,*
> *and the messages of prophets like Genevieve,*
> *we thank you.*
Please give us
> *good ears to listen,*
> *good minds to understand,*
> *and good feet and hands to follow and to do your will.*
Amen.

The Maiden Who Gave Things Away

SAINT BRIGID
A.D. 450–523

ext to Patrick, Brigid is probably the most honored saint in Ireland. Patrick was an old man by the time she was born, and Christianity had already spread to her Ulster homeland in the north of Ireland. She was a beautiful young girl, so the stories go, who decided very early to give her life wholly to God, and who fulfilled that promise through a lifetime's service to the poor.

Patrick's preaching had already changed the people of Ireland, and during her lifetime, Brigid would see it change the shape of Ireland's landscape as well. In her youth, there were no cities in Ireland, just scattered farmers and herdsmen ruled by local kings—the Kingdom of Ulster, the Kingdom of Leinster (LEN-ster), the Kingdom of Meath. But through Patrick's teaching, Irish Christians learned about the Desert Fathers (Moses and John—remember?), and soon set off to follow their example. Many formed monastic communities— places of compassion and learning and prayer. People flocked to these communities, and the monasteries—as they were called—became the beginnings of the first Irish cities.

Monks weren't the only people founding these little communities. There were women, as well, whose lives were so good and inspiring that crowds also gathered around them.

BRIGID COULDN'T HELP IT.

Ever since she'd heard about Jesus, she had been determined to do whatever was necessary to follow him. The poor, the blind, the outcast, the lame—Jesus helped them all. And that's all Brigid wanted to do. But her father just didn't understand.

He was rich. His barns were full of grain. So what did it matter if she borrowed some of it, now and then, and gave it to the poor?

Brigid's father had had enough!

Maybe this new religion of Brigid's had made her a more kind and compassionate young woman, but it was going to ruin him. She was strong-willed and stubborn, and no amount of arguing was going to keep her from emptying his barns.

She had to go. It was as simple as that. So one fresh, green Irish morning, he tossed her in the back of his chariot and sped off across the country.

"Where are we going?" Brigid asked.

"To see the king of Leinster," he grunted. "It's come down to this: I can't have you giving away any more of my grain. So I'm giving *you* away instead. You must do whatever the king tells you. Work in his fields or his flour mills, and put that energy of yours to some good use."

Brigid was sad. "I *have* been putting my energy to good use!" she thought. But she said nothing, and soon they were outside the home of the king of Leinster.

"Wait here," her father commanded. He took off his sword and belt and carefully placed them on the floor of the chariot.

"A sign of peace," he explained, "no weapons in the king's home." Then he marched off to see the king.

While Brigid was waiting near the chariot, a man with leprosy happened by—sick and penniless and hungry.

"I don't suppose you could help me?" he asked.

And it was all Brigid could do to keep the tears from running down her pretty face.

"I'm so sorry," she said "so very sorry. But I have no money or food or anything to give you."

"I understand," the man sighed. "It's what everyone says." And he started to walk away.

"No . . . no . . . it's true! I really don't!" Brigid called. Then she sadly hung her head. Jesus would have helped. And she was sad and embarrassed that she could not. Now the tears really did begin to flow, and her red hair fell like a veil across her face.

And that's when she saw it. Through her hair and through her tears she spotted her father's sword lying on the chariot floor.

"Wait!" she cried. "I do have something I can give you after all."

The man with leprosy turned and limped back to the chariot, and Brigid handed him her father's sword.

"You can keep it," she said. "Or sell it and buy yourself some food."

The man could not believe his luck.

"Thank you!" he said. And again, "Thank you! Thank you very much!" Then he hobbled off into the forest clutching his newfound treasure.

Brigid stood there beaming, her pretty face fresh-washed with tears, her crimson hair like a waterfall around her shoulders, her eyes shining bright as sunlight on the sea.

And that's how her father and the king of Leinster found her when they came out to the chariot.

"She's a beautiful maiden!" the king remarked.

"What did I tell you?" grinned Brigid's father. "A good, strong worker, too. Or, who knows, maybe even a lovely wife for one of your sons. So what do you say?"

"It's a hard offer to pass by," said the king. "But what I really want to know is this: Why would anyone want to part with such a girl?"

Before Brigid's father had the chance to answer, however, he glanced into the chariot—and noticed that his sword was gone!

"Brigid," he asked, in as polite a tone as he could muster, "Brigid, what happened to my sword?"

"Oh, Father!" she exclaimed, "don't you know that's why I'm standing here as happy as any Christian girl could be? A poor leper came by—he was so hungry and sad, Father—and I couldn't help myself. I really couldn't!"

"So . . . you gave him my . . . sword?" her father stammered. "*You gave away my sword?!*" And he raised his hand to strike her.

"Stop!" the king commanded, and he gazed at the girl in wonder.

"I have to know," he said. "Why would you take your father's sword—his most valued possession—and give it away to a beggar?"

Brigid looked back at the king with a strength and a shining in her eyes that he had seen only in his most valiant foes.

Then she grinned. "If it was up to me," she said, "I would empty your house as well and give your treasures to the poor brothers and sisters of Jesus."

"I see," said the king. Then he turned to Brigid's father. "I'm afraid I'm going to have to turn down your offer, my friend. Your daughter is as willful as she is beautiful, and I am afraid that such a combination would mean nothing but trouble for myself and my young princes."

The king returned to his house, and Brigid's father just stood there shaking his head. His sword was gone. The king was gone. But the daughter he had tried so hard to leave behind was still with him.

"Don't be upset, Father," Brigid said with a smile. "I have an idea. For a long while now, it has been my desire to go off to some wooded place, build a little hut, and serve the poor and sick in

Jesus' name. Bishop Patrick said it was a good thing to do, and there are many young men and women all around our land who have already committed themselves to such a life. With your permission, I would like to join them."

Brigid's father smiled a relieved smile. "And you promise to stay away from my barns?" he asked.

"I promise," she grinned. "Unless, of course, you'd like to make a donation to my work!"

So Brigid left her father and built a little hut in the shade of a giant oak tree. Everyone who came by was touched by her hospitality, and soon there were many more huts. Then a village. Then a town. Then at last one of Ireland's very first cities—a place called Kildare, where the poor, the blind, the outcast, and the lame all got what they needed in Jesus' name.

Kildare actually means "giant oak," and under the shade of that oak, Brigid established what would be called a "double monastery," a community where both men and women were welcome. Brigid served as abbess— or leader—of both the women and men, a situation that would have seemed peculiar to any Christian visiting from Rome. For there, as in most of the Christian world, women were not permitted to have authority over men.

But then, Irish Christianity, or Celtic (KEL-tick) Christianity as it came to be called, was always a little different from the rest. Women were given a more prominent place. So was nature. Perhaps because there was so much beauty around them, Irish Christians gave special attention to the glory of God as it was revealed to them through birds and beasts and flowers and fields. And more than that, they even adapted what they had learned about their faith to their own particular surroundings. The Celtic symbol for the Holy Spirit, for example, is not a gentle dove, but a wild goose!

Finally, inspired by that wild goose, those early Celtic Christians developed a whole new kind of "martyrdom." In the early days of the church, persecution like Marcella faced resulted in the deaths of many Christians. There was no persecution in Ireland, however. Patrick's revolution was a peaceful one—on both sides. So the Irish monks came up with a kind of martyrdom—a witness to their faith—that was all their own. They left their lovely island voluntarily to sail across the waters in tiny boats called coracles in order to spread the gospel to other lands, just as Patrick had brought it to them.

These monks took their Christian faith to the Picts in what is now Scotland, and to the Angles and Saxons who were moving from Denmark and Norway into the north of England. Then they moved onto the European continent itself, sharing the gospel with the nations that had displaced the power of Rome. Some went to Iceland and Greenland as well; and if we are to believe the stories about Brendan the Navigator, some even landed on the shores of North America.

For the Irish, the Holy Spirit was a wild goose, indeed—who sent them migrating across the world, honking and hymning the praises of God!

Talk about It

- Do you think there was anything wrong with Brigid giving her father's grain to the poor or his sword to the man with leprosy? How do you think your parents would feel if you gave their VCR or pool table or lawnmower to needy people?

- Do you know anyone who is stubborn and strong-willed like Brigid was? Can you think of a situation where those attributes would be helpful, and another situation where they might not be as useful? Can you think of any people in the Bible who were stubborn?

Prayer

Here is part of a mealtime prayer traditionally connected to Brigid:

God bless the poor,
God bless the sick,
And bless our human race.
God bless our food,
God bless our drink,
All homes, O God, embrace.
Amen.

A Song in the Stable

SAINT HILDA OF WHITBY
A.D. 614–680

W hen Hilda was just a baby, her father was poisoned by one of his enemies, a rival king. As Hilda's mother grieved for her slain husband, she dreamed that she found a precious jewel hidden beneath her clothes. She stared at the jewel when suddenly light burst from it and shone through all the land!

That precious jewel was her daughter Hilda. Hilda lived a godly life among her noble friends and family—in spite of the fact that Christians were persecuted at the time. When she was thirty-three, she felt God's call to enter a monastery. Later, she was made abbess and sent to lead a small monastery at a nearby town. Finally, she was sent to establish a brand new monastery on a cliff high above the North Sea, at the town of Whitby on England's east coast.

There she stayed for the rest of her life, building a community dedicated to learning, holiness, and peace. Whitby was a "double monastery," open to men and women alike. Because of Hilda's noble "connections," it was often visited by kings and nobles. But the monastery was also home to the poor.

The dream of Hilda's mother came true. For in the darkest time of a dark, dark age, shone the light of knowledge and peace and hope—even for one so poor and unknown as a stable-hand named Caedmon (KAD-mun).

CAEDMON WAS AN OLD MAN—a stable-hand who cared for horses and cows and did odd jobs around his master's farm.

He was good with his hands. He was quick on his feet. And he could groom a horse or milk a cow as well as anyone. But there was one thing Caedmon could not do—he could not sing.

And that is why, on the night of the annual harvest feast, Caedmon was sitting by himself in a corner of the stable while the rest of his master's servants were enjoying themselves in the great dining hall.

According to custom, the harp had gone around the room. "Sing us a song!" the crowd had demanded as each person was handed the harp. And each, in turn, had sung: silly songs, heroic songs, sad and long and weepy songs. But when the harp had come to Caedmon, he had frozen, too frightened to hum even a single note. And then he had run—he was still quick on his feet—out the dining hall, across the farmyard, and into the safety of his stable.

"Why can't I do it?" he moaned to the horses.

"Won't you please help me?" he cried to God. "Help me find the courage to sing like everybody else."

And then he fell asleep, curled up in the corner and bedded down in hay, with the distant music of the feast dancing in his ears.

Midnight came and went. Then one and two o'clock. And Caedmon began to dream. He saw a figure, then a face, and finally a mouth that opened up and spoke his name.

"Caedmon," the figure said gently, "Caedmon, sing me a song."

"I can't sing," Caedmon sighed. "That's why I left the feast."

"I know," said the figure, more gently still. "You were afraid to sing for them. But there are only the two of us here. Surely you can sing for me."

"But I don't know any songs," explained Caedmon. "What would I sing about?"

The figure looked around—at the stable straw, at the farmyard birds, at the slumbering horses and cows. "Sing about what you know," he said. "Sing about the creation of all things!"

And so Caedmon began to sing.

The words came from somewhere deep inside, rushing up his throat and tumbling out from his lips. And these were the words he began to sing:

Praise we the Fashioner now of Heaven's fabric,
The majesty of his might and his mind's wisdom,
Work of the world-warden, worker of all wonders,
How he the Lord of Glory everlasting,
Wrought first for the race of men Heaven as a rooftree,
Then made he Middle Earth to be their mansion . . .

When the song had finished, Caedmon awoke. The figure was gone, and the rooster on the roof was just about to launch into his own morning wake-up song.

Caedmon ran the lines of the song over and over again in his head. He remembered every word! Then he set off to find his master.

"Begging your pardon, sir," said Caedmon, "but I have something very important to tell you."

"If it's about last night," his master said with a smile, "there is no need to worry. Everyone knows you don't like to sing."

"But that's just it, sir," Caedmon interrupted, "I know how to sing now. I *want* to sing. And I have a special song I want you to hear!"

Then that song came tumbling out of Caedmon's mouth again. And it was all the master or his wife or the rest of the servants could do to hold back their tears—so beautiful was the melody, so deep and true the words.

"Where did you hear this song?" the master demanded to know.

"In my dream," said Caedmon. "I saw a figure. He asked me to sing. I suppose it was from him that the song came."

"I've never heard anything so beautiful before, Caedmon," the master said. "I suspect it was God himself who gave you that song. And that's why we're going to the monastery."

And off they went along the River Esk to the sea.

"If anyone can tell us where your song came from," the master explained, "it's Mother Hilda. A more peaceful or charitable soul you'll never meet. She loves God. And she knows God's ways as well as any man or woman can. If she can't help us, nobody can."

"But will she see me?" asked Caedmon. "They say she's a noble-woman. And I'm just an old stable-hand."

"That makes no difference to her now," the master answered. "Everyone is welcome at the monastery—men and women, rich and poor alike. And all are treated equally. You'll see for yourself soon enough. Look, there's the place now!"

Caedmon raised his head, and there it was—standing on a cliff three hundred feet above the spot where the river emptied into the sea. It stood proud and dark against the slate grey autumn sky. But from its windows shone a golden light of such warmth that Caedmon could not wait to get there.

"One more thing," he asked as the master knocked at the door, "do you think the abbess will like the poem—what with it being in English and all? I mean, it's not in that fancy language the priests and their like speak."

"Latin," the master said. "Well, noble people—people of learning—may speak Latin among themselves, but they understand our language well enough, too. We'll just have to wait and see."

The door opened, and the golden light that Caedmon had seen from the road now poured all over him.

Caedmon's master explained the situation to the monk who welcomed them, and as soon as he heard, he hurried off to find the abbess.

The monk returned quickly and asked the pair to follow him. "You're in luck," he explained. "Mother Hilda is hosting a gathering of scholars and monks from across the country. They know the scriptures well and are eager to hear your song."

They were led into a large round room full of people. At the front sat Mother Hilda, looking for all the world like the monastery itself—tall and strong and noble. A warm look shone from her eyes, and Caedmon felt instantly at ease.

"I understand God has given you a song," she said to Caedmon in her very best English. And then she smiled. "Would you like to share it with us?"

The old man nodded and swallowed. Then he opened his mouth and sang.

And it was all any of them could do to keep the tears from rolling down their faces.

"It's beautiful!" someone said.

"It's inspired!" said someone else.

"But . . . it's . . . in . . . English!" said someone from the back of the room.

And that's when Mother Hilda spoke.

"Indeed it is in English!" she beamed. "And that makes it all the more special. For through it God speaks to us all—not just to those of learning, but to all of us, in the language of our land!"

Then she took Caedmon aside and spoke to him gently. "God has given you a gift, and I would like to help you develop and use it. Would you like to stay at the monastery?"

Caedmon looked around nervously. "But my master . . ." he said. "And my animals."

"I know your master well," Mother Hilda replied. "And I am sure he will do what is best for you. As for the animals, we have plenty here you could care for while you learn the scriptures and write your songs."

So Caedmon happily agreed. He went to live at the monastery. With every section of scripture he learned—every story, every psalm, every commandment—Caedmon composed a song.

And with the help of Mother Hilda, the man who could not stand up and sing in front of a crowd became the very first English poet!

*A*nd so it was that Hilda of Whitby became, not only the founder of a famous monastery, but also the Mother of English Literature.

Whitby, by the way, is the name of the English fishing village where you can find the ruins of Hilda's monastery, as well as what some people say is the grave of old Caedmon. The Danes gave it the name of Whitby when they invaded the place many years after Hilda's death. But in her day, the place was called Streanashalch (STRAN-a-shock), an old word that meant, appropriately, "the light of the beacon"!

Talk about It

- Think of someone who has been a source of encouragement to you—a teacher, maybe, or a pastor or a coach. How did that person encourage you? What did that person say or do to help you improve yourself?

- In his New Testament letter to the church at Rome, the apostle Paul writes that God has given special gifts to all Christians. Caedmon's gift was his poetry. What gift do you think God has given you? And how can you use that gift to help others?

Prayer

Dear God,
Thank you for making each one of us different, special, unique. Thank you for the gifts and talents you have given us. Help us to find them— like you helped Caedmon—and show us how to use them in ways that please you and serve others. Amen.

Alone at Last!

SAINT CUTHBERT
A.D. 634–687

*e don't always get what we want. More than anything, Cuthbert wanted to be a hermit—a monk, like some of the Desert Fathers—who lived by himself and spent his life reading scripture, thinking about God, and praying.*

But God had different plans. He knew Cuthbert was an excellent teacher. He knew Cuthbert had a kind and generous heart. So instead of sending Cuthbert to a place where he was far from people, God placed him right in their midst—in a monastery at Melrose, in what is now Scotland but what was then the kingdom of Northumberland.

Cuthbert traveled on horseback all over Northumberland. And wherever he went, crowds would gather. Some came to listen to his teaching. Others came to be healed and blessed by his prayers. Still others came to confess their sins and set their lives right with God. And they all came in hopes of seeing one of the monk's famous miracles.

A baby healed with a kiss. Sailors saved from a stormy sea. The people had heard reports, and they wanted to see a miracle for themselves. But all Cuthbert wanted was to be alone. Alone with God. Alone with God's creation. Alone with his thoughts and prayers So that is what he sought one dark night at the monastery in Coldingham, where he had gone to preach and teach. But, once again, God had something different in mind.

CUTHBERT SAT UP, then stood up and stretched. It was midnight and everyone else was asleep. Every monk. Every nun. Even Mother Abb, who had invited him to the monastery at Coldingham to teach and encourage the religious community there.

It had been a long day, and Cuthbert had slept only a few hours. He was still very tired. But the opportunity to be by himself—to pray and think about God—was so important to him that he shoved that tiredness aside like an old wool blanket.

Cuthbert slipped on his rough monk's robe and his worn leather sandals and crept out of his room.

It's not that he disliked people. It was just that the job God had called him to demanded that he be with them almost all the time— counseling the monks at his home monastery in Melrose, visiting the poor and sick people around the countryside. He loved all that, he really did. But there was good to be found in being alone as well. And right now that's what Cuthbert craved.

So he tiptoed along the dark corridors until he found his way outside. Just as he stepped through the doorway, something rattled behind him. The door on its latch? Some sleep-starved rat, perhaps? Whatever it was, Cuthbert paid it little heed. Finally, Cuthbert was alone!

Or so he thought.

For at that very same moment, young Erc, gangly Erc, forever-tripping-and-stumbling Erc, was rubbing his stubbed toe and berating himself for having decided to secretly follow Cuthbert on his midnight outing.

It had seemed like a good idea when the sun was shining.

"If you want to be a good monk," his friend Trumwine had told him, "you have to follow the best possible example."

"Well, what better example was there than Cuthbert?" thought Erc. A great teacher and leader and miracle worker. And then there were the rumors. He'd heard whispers that Cuthbert would go off by himself to pray all night and the most spectacular things would happen. Why, one night, they said, Cuthbert had even seen the soul of the great bishop Aidan (AY-dun) meet up with angels in the sky!

That's the kind of thing Erc wanted to see. So on he crept, trying as hard as he could not to make any more noise.

He followed Cuthbert out the front door and the front monastery gates, then down the rocky coast to the sea. Erc tried to be quiet. He really did. But between the driftwood and the seaweed and the pebbly beach, he couldn't help slipping and stumbling and tripping a time or two.

Cuthbert stopped several times to listen. And Erc stood stone-still, praying that the monk would not turn around. His prayers were answered. And finally he ducked behind the wreckage of an old fishing boat; from there he was able to watch, unnoticed, as Cuthbert walked straight into the cold North Sea!

The waves washed up to Cuthbert's ankles. Then his knees. They washed over his waist and his chest. And when they rolled right up to his armpits, the monk raised his hands high, threw back his head, and began to pray.

Cuthbert was filled with a joy he could not describe. The biting sea. The hard bright stars. The chuckling waves. The gull songs. The cry of a dolphin far away. Overwhelmed by the wonder of God's creation, he drew near to God himself, and the passing of that night seemed no longer to him than an hour.

But for Erc things were very different. First, he was freezing. Then he just couldn't get comfortable. He was sitting on something—an odd-shaped stone maybe, or a dried-up starfish. And the more he wriggled, the more uncomfortable he became.

He tried to keep his eyes on Cuthbert. But his sore bottom and frozen toes argued that he should give this all up, hobble back to the monastery, and climb into his warm bed.

"No!" Erc argued with himself. "I'm here to watch, and I'll stay as long as Cuthbert does!"

Finally, however, Erc's eyelids joined the argument and, try as he might, they could not be persuaded from dropping like two doors over his weary eyes.

Several hours later, Erc awoke as the sun stuck its shining head over the eastern edge of the sea. The waves shone and sparkled in reply and kept Erc, at first, from finding the figure of Cuthbert. The old monk had turned around now, his back to the sun, and was walking slowly out of the water.

"Oh no!" moaned Erc. "I've fallen asleep. I've seen nothing! And all I've got to show for my troubles is a sore back and a runny nose."

The waves dropped below Cuthbert's chest, then his belly, then his knees. But when the waves rolled right down to Cuthbert's ankles, Erc saw something, or rather two somethings—two dark and sleek somethings swimming on either side of the monk.

Erc rubbed his eyes and looked closer. Otters! That's what they were! And when Cuthbert stepped out of the sea, the otters stepped out with him. They rolled over his feet, tumbling and twisting, warming the monk's feet with their breath until they were dry!

Cuthbert smiled and reached down to pat the otters on their heads.

"Thank you, friends," he said. Then he sent them off with a blessing and started back up the beach to the monastery.

Erc followed slowly, a great distance behind—partly because his legs were stiff and cold, and partly because he was staggering with amazement.

He'd come to witness a miracle, and, sure enough, he'd seen one! A very minor miracle, granted, but a miracle nonetheless. What should he do now? If he told anyone—even someone like Trumwine—Cuthbert might discover that Erc had been spying on him. He wouldn't want that. No, Erc would keep this to himself. And he'd get back to the monastery as fast as he could.

Cuthbert returned first, of course, and slipped into the morning prayer service quietly so no one would notice he was a bit late. He'd changed his robe. He looked warm and dry. But, once again, things were very different for poor Erc.

Perhaps it was the excitement. Or the cold. Or maybe it was just that tall, awkward Erc found it impossible to quietly slip in anywhere. As he entered the prayer service, he slipped and stumbled and tripped so that no one could help but notice he was late.

What's more, his clothes were still damp with the night air and heavy with the salty smell of the sea. Cuthbert looked at Erc. Erc looked back sheepishly at Cuthbert. When the prayer service had finished, the older monk turned to the young one.

"You were watching me last night, weren't you?" Cuthbert asked.

"Yes, yes, I was," admitted Erc. The he fell in a heap at Cuthbert's feet. "Please forgive me!" he begged. "I only wanted to become a better monk. Well," and this he said a little more quietly, "and maybe to see a miracle or two."

"I see," said Cuthbert. "So the otters . . ."

"Yes, the otters!" exclaimed Erc. "They were wonderful, weren't they?"

"They were indeed." Cuthbert smiled at last. "Even when we are alone—or *think* we are alone—God finds some way to take care of us. And make us useful to someone else, I suppose. Listen," he said quietly, "I'm not angry. There's nothing to forgive. But let me ask you this: Can we keep this little incident between ourselves? Make it our secret? After all, I don't want every young monk in the monastery following me out to sea at night."

"Of course," Erc agreed, grinning and climbing to his feet. "Absolutely! Whatever you say!"

"Good," said Cuthbert. "Thank you." Then, just like he'd done with the otters, he gently put his hand on Erc's head and gave him a blessing.

Erc stumbled off down the hall to change his clothes. And he kept his promise to Cuthbert. Well, at least until after Cuthbert died. Then he told Trumwine. And Trumwine told Aelfrid (AL-frid). And Aelfrid told someone else, until eventually the story came to a monk named Bede (BEAD), who wrote it all down. Which is a good thing really. For otherwise, we wouldn't be able to enjoy it now!

*B*ede was the author of A History of the English Church and People, *written fifty years or so after Cuthbert died. The book covers the history of the church in Britain from its beginnings up to Bede's own time, and it is our main source of information on both Cuthbert and another remarkable saint named Hilda of Whitby. Bede was also a monk who served in a Northumberland monastery, and he tells us that Cuthbert finally got what he wanted.*

When he was thirty, Cuthbert moved from Melrose to the monastery at Lindisfarne (LIN-dis-farn), on the east coast of what is now northern England. Twelve years later, he was given permission to live by himself, not far away, on a tiny island called Farne. There he built a little hut, dug a well, and grew a few crops. He raised a wall around that hut so that all he could see were the heavens above. Then he read and he thought and he prayed—just like he had always dreamed of doing.

Eight years later, however, God's plans interrupted Cuthbert's solitude once again. The bishop of Lindisfarne died, and the king's choice for his replacement was, of course, Cuthbert! So he went back to the monastery to again serve both God and God's people. Two years later, he returned to his beloved island, where he died a short time later.

Talk about It

- Throughout the history of the church, some monks have served God as hermits—all alone—while others have spent their lives working with people. Talk about the advantages and disadvantages of each kind of service. Which do you think would be harder for you?

- You might like to set aside time each day for a week or a month, maybe, to be by yourself with God. Go to some beautiful spot if there is one near and the weather permits. Or just go to a place that's quiet and peaceful—a place that makes you feel good. Talk to God, read your Bible, and take the time to just think. See if you don't grow closer to God that way, just like Cuthbert did.

Prayer

Dear God,
Thank you for the times when we are alone and for the times when we can be with other people. When we are alone, draw us close to you and fill us with your love, so that when we are with others, we can pass that love along. Amen.

The Bishop and the Sword

SAINT STANISLAS
A.D. 1030–1079

he power of the church. The power of the king. In eleventh-century Poland, those powers were pretty clearly separated. The king was responsible for defending the country, keeping the peace, collecting the taxes, and, hopefully, ruling over his subjects with justice and honor.

The church was responsible for the spiritual health of the nation, encouraging goodness and mercy and holiness among Poland's people. And the church was responsible for questions of "eternity" as well. To be "in the church" was to be on the road to heaven, while to be "out of the church" meant a much "warmer" eternal stay!

The power of the church. The power of the king. What happened when those powers disagreed? That was the problem Stanislas (STAN-i-sloss) faced. A popular preacher and pastor, he was appointed Bishop of Krakow, the capital of Poland, in 1072. Unfortunately, Boleslas (BOHL-a-sloss) II, king of Poland at the time, was not a kind and just ruler, but a wicked and vicious tyrant. And when he kidnapped the wife of a nobleman and took her as his own, Bishop Stanislas knew there was only one thing that could happen: the "powers" would have to clash.

STANISLAS CLOSED THE BIBLE, shut his eyes, and buried his face in his hands. The story he had read could have been his own—word for word, character for character, problem for problem. David, king of Israel, had sinned. He had taken Bathsheba, another man's wife, for his own. And then he had arranged to have that man killed in battle.

And what did God do? God sent his servant, the prophet Nathan, to confront the king with his sin and lead him to feel sorrow and repentance for what he had done.

It was a dangerous job telling a king that he was wrong. Nathan could have been imprisoned or banished or killed right there and then. A dangerous job, indeed—a fact Stanislas knew well, for the same job was facing him.

Stanislas was the bishop of Krakow. Krakow was the capital of Poland. And Poland was ruled by King Boleslas II, a cruel and will-ful monarch who, like King David, had just run off with another man's wife.

Some bishops might have ignored this behavior either out of fear or in the hopes of receiving some royal reward. But Stanislas was not like those bishops. He took his responsibilities seriously. If any other Christian in Krakow had done such a sinful thing, he would have tried to correct him and lead him to repentance. So why should he treat the king differently? Why should the king be above God's law simply because he was the king?

No, Stanislas could not chase the story of Nathan and King David out of his mind. God was speaking to him through that story. And, just like Nathan, he would have to face the danger. He would have to face the king! The next day, Stanislas found himself in the throne room, head bowed before King Boleslas.

"Your Majesty," said the bishop, "I come to you on a matter of some . . . delicacy." Then he glanced at the guards gathered around the throne. "It might be best if we were alone."

King Boleslas thought for a moment and then grinned.

"Of course!" he said. "Why not? I think it highly unlikely that my bishop has come here to assassinate me. Guards!" he ordered. "The bishop and I would like to be alone!"

Stanislas did his best. He told the king that what he had done was wrong. He explained that it was not a good example for the people. He begged him to send the woman back to her husband. But with each sentence, Stanislas could see the king's mood grow darker and darker.

Surely, he thought, this was not how King David's face had looked as he listened to the prophet Nathan.

"I thought you meant me no harm," said the king at last, "but your words cut deeper than any assassin's knife." Then, rising from his throne, he continued. "Just who do you think you are?" the king shouted. "I am Boleslas, king of all Poland! And you . . . you are nothing more than a priest in fancy dress. Yet you dare to tell me what to do?"

"Not I, Your Majesty," answered Stanislas, "but God. It is God who says that you are wrong."

"Then let God come and tell me himself!" the king shouted even more loudly. "But until I hear from him, I shall stay with the woman I love. Now go! And remember your place!"

Stanislas went. Back to his house. Back to his Bible. Back to his prayers. But the more he prayed and the more he read, the more convinced he was that he should see the king again.

"Perhaps I was not clear enough," he thought. "Or perhaps I was not kind enough. After all, it is hard for any man to hear that he is wrong—much less a king. I shall give him another chance."

So the very next day, Stanislas found himself in the throne room again.

"Your Majesty . . ." he began. But before he could say another word, the king interrupted him.

"No need to continue," the king smiled; "I understand perfectly. Yesterday, you let your religion get in the way of your patriotism and your common sense. You're sorry for that and for any injury you may have done me. And now you've come to apologize. Well, Bishop Stanislas, apology accepted!"

Stanislas just stood there open-mouthed. That was not what he had intended to say at all!

"Your Majesty," he answered softly, "I think you misunderstand me. I did not come here to apologize. I came to give you another chance. Change your ways. Repent of your sin. Send the woman back to her husband. And I am sure God will forgive you."

Now it was the king's turn to stare open-mouthed.

"I cannot believe my ears!" the king growled. "I have been understanding. I have been patient. And I have offered you an honorable way out of the uncomfortable situation you placed us in. But still you insist on insulting me and sticking your nose where it does not belong!"

"But, Your Majesty," Stanislas pleaded, "this is exactly where it belongs! I am bishop of this city, responsible for the spiritual health of every Christian in it—yourself included. And I would be ignoring my duty, both to God and to you, if I did not bring this to your attention."

And then the bishop paused and looked very solemnly at his king.

"I want more than anything for you to repent and receive God's forgiveness. But if you do not, then I shall have to treat you exactly as I would treat anyone who turned his back on God's will. I will have to put you out of the church."

"Put me out of the church?!" King Boleslas roared. "Excommunicate me? *But I am the king!*"

"And I am the bishop," Stanislas replied in a firm but quiet voice, "which means that I have every right to put you out of the church. And I will do it if you will not change your ways."

The king slammed his fist on the throne. "Get out!" he shouted. "Get out before I throw you out!"

"I will go," answered Stanislas, "but in three days I will return. And if you have not changed your mind by then, it is I who will be throwing *you* out—out of the church and away from God's forgiveness."

Stanislas left, leaving the angry king pacing back and forth across the throne-room floor.

"I will not be thrown out of the church!" he muttered. "It would weaken my standing with the army and the noblemen, and they would lose respect for me. But I will not lose my woman, either!

"Lose the church or lose the woman. That is the choice that meddling bishop has left me." And then the king sat down on his throne and smiled a wicked smile.

"But there is a third choice," he mused aloud. "A choice that he has not considered . . ."

The king thought long and hard about that third choice. And finally he decided. It is unlikely that Boleslas knew much at all about King David, but he was about to become like that biblical king in one more way. A horrible way. His sinful love for a woman would lead him to murder.

First he sent his guards to do the deed—late that evening while Stanislas was leading a service in the church. Three times they crept in, intent on killing the bishop. But three times they returned, frightened by a bright light that glowed around Stanislas.

"I shall have to do this myself," the king snarled at last. Taking a sword from one of his guards, he marched into the church.

"Get out! All of you!" he ordered the congregation. "I need to speak to the bishop!"

When they had gone, Boleslas marched to the front of the building, right up to the altar. At first, Stanislas thought he was there to ask forgiveness, and he rejoiced that the king was finally ready to surrender to God. But when he saw the sword and the dark look on the king's face, Stanislas understood that surrender was the furthest thing from the monarch's mind.

"You left me with two choices, priest!" the king sneered. "Lose the church or lose the woman. Well I am here to tell you I have made a third choice. I have decided to lose . . . the bishop!"

And with that, he grabbed Stanislas by the throat and drove his sword deep into the bishop's chest.

Stanislas died instantly. Once Boleslas had wiped his sword clean, he marched back out of the church.

So this clash between church and king was resolved in a most tragic way. The bishop lay dead, a willing sacrifice in front of the altar. And the king, having added murder to the list of evils he had committed, walked away from his sins and from the only place where he could find forgiveness.

*E*ventually, Stanislas became one of the most revered of Poland's saints. Perhaps that is because the powers of church and government in Poland continued to come into conflict. As recently as the 1980s, for example, the people of Poland struggled against what was then a communist government for the right to have labor unions. People died in that struggle, and among the dead were priests who stood for what was right and just—like Stanislas did— and paid the same awful price.

Talk about It

- If Stanislas had just "minded his own business," he would not have been killed. Did he *have* to tell the king he was wrong? Could he have handled the situation in another way?

- In his New Testament letter to the Galatian Christians, the apostle Paul says we should try to correct someone who is doing something wrong, but that we should do it gently, keeping our own faults in mind as well. Have you ever tried to stop someone from doing what was wrong? Talk about what happened—how it felt and whether or not you were successful.

Prayer

Dear God,
When we follow Jesus, we become citizens of two kingdoms—
the Kingdom of Heaven and the country in which we live. When
those two kingdoms disagree, help us to say and to do what pleases
you, with gentleness and courage, with honesty and with love. Amen.

The Stranger in the Cave

SAINT MARGARET OF SCOTLAND
A.D. 1045–1083

ho wouldn't want to be a princess? Castles, ladies-in-waiting, the chance to marry a handsome prince.

But it wasn't so easy for Princess Margaret. Her grandfather was one of the earliest and most beloved kings of England. And her father was next in line for the throne. It was expected that she should marry some prince and cement an alliance. But Margaret wanted to lead a religious life and give herself totally to the service of God.

When her father died and England was conquered by the Frenchman William of Normandy, everything changed for Margaret. Her life was in danger. To escape William, Margaret and her family sought refuge from her father's old ally, Malcolm, king of Scotland.

Malcolm was wild and savage, not a prince young princesses dream of, but this didn't keep him from asking for Margaret's hand in marriage.

Margaret prayed about it and, at the age of twenty-three, she married Malcolm and then set about changing both the king and the land he ruled. She encouraged him to treat his people more justly. She introduced English "comforts" like wall tapestries and window glass into his cold and damp castles. But, more than anything, she longed for Malcolm to abandon his pagan religion and follow Jesus. To that end she prayed—day after day and night after night.

MALCOLM, KING OF SCOTLAND, rubbed his sleepy eyes and swung his hairy legs out of bed. It was the middle of the night, and someone was knocking at his door.

"It's me, Your Majesty," whispered that someone. "It's Callum."

Malcolm yanked open the door and stared sleepily at one of his court advisors. Unlike the king, Callum was wide awake and fully dressed.

"There's no time to waste!" said Callum, eager as a hound on the heels of a rabbit. "She's gone. And if we don't hurry, we'll have no chance of catching her!"

"Aye," the king sighed, shaking his shaggy head. "I suppose we have to follow. I just have trouble believing it, that's all."

"But you must!" Callum pleaded. "Every week, for a month now, the queen has disappeared into the forest and remained there all night. My men have seen her go. They have seen her return. Now you tell me: Why would any woman do that if she were not . . ."

". . . seeing another man," said Malcolm, wincing as he finished the sentence. "Aye. You're right. There can be no other reason."

Slowly the king pulled on his leggings and his tunic and his boots. But what was hardest to wear was the ill-fitting possibility that his wife could ever be unfaithful to him.

"She loves me. I know it," he said, trying hard to convince both himself and his advisor. "And besides, her religion would never allow it."

"Her religion?" Callum sneered. "The religion of the English, you mean. Well, as far as I can tell, Christianity has not made any of them more trustworthy. Why should it do the same for her?"

"Enough, Callum!" the king snapped. "I'll not have you speaking against my wife's faith nor her kinsmen. Stick to your duties and help me find the woman."

"As you wish, sir. But we had better hurry if we're going to catch her."

So off they went, Callum and the king, out of the castle and into the Forest of Dunfermline (dun-FIRM-lun). It was a wet night, cold and foggy, and it was all Callum could do to spot the guards he'd set to mark the queen's progress.

"To the north, sir," said one guard.

"Past that tree, sir," said the next.

"Down the hill, sir, and up the other side," said a third.

And on they went, past guard after guard, tracing the nighttime journey of the queen—the two men silent, embraced by the fog and their very different questions and thoughts.

"At last," Callum thought to himself, "at last we will be rid of her! She had no right to be here in the first place. An English princess wed to a Scottish king? Ridiculous! And her English 'ways'—I'm sick to death of them. Tapestries on the walls. Plates on the table. Glass in the windows. We're Scotsmen, not little girls. We've no use for such fancies and fineries. The king is so in love, he just can't see it. Well, he'll see it now—with his own eyes—just as soon as we've found her with that other man!"

Malcolm, however, was thinking far sadder thoughts.

"A wee lass. A wee bonnie lass. That's all she was when she came to me. She and her mother and her brother on the run from William, conqueror and new king of England.

"I took them in. I treated them well. And I never said she had to marry me. She wanted to. She said so.

"I'm no fool. I know what everyone must think. She's young and beautiful and as smart as anyone I've ever met. And I'm old and rough and can neither read nor write. What could she possibly see in me?

"Well, one thing's sure: the man she's with may be smarter than me, and he may be younger, too. But when I catch him, I'll cut him to pieces! And Margaret had better pray I don't do the same to her as well."

A voice from the fog interrupted the king's sad and angry thoughts.

"She went into the cave, sir," said the guard. "It's just over there."

"Shall I go first, Your Majesty?" suggested Callum. "Just in case the man is armed."

"You'll not go at all," snapped the king. "She's my wife, and it's my duty to take care of this!"

"But, Your Majesty," Callum protested, "what about my duty? If anything should happen to you in that cave, I could never forgive myself."

"All right," the king sighed. Then he pointed his finger at his advisor. "But I shall take the lead!"

Quietly they crept across the forest floor, and then into the cave's black mouth. Fern and fog gave way to dripping walls and darkness as they stumbled forward like blind men, their hands stretched out in front of their faces. At last, they saw it—the tiniest spark of light.

"That'll be her torch," the king whispered. "Careful, now. Listen."

All they could hear was mumbling at first. So they dropped to their hands and knees and crawled even closer. Soon they could understand an occasional word.

"Please . . ."

"I beg you . . ."

And then the words "I love you" came tumbling out of the darkness to crush the king's heart.

"What did I tell you, Your Majesty?" Callum hissed. "She's declaring her love for the man even now!"

"Quiet!" the king growled, low and lion-like. Then he reached for his sword and crept closer still. "A few more feet and this man will be no more!"

But in those few feet, the queen's words became perfectly clear—clear as a torch in a deep black cave.

"I love you, Lord," she said. "But I love him, too. More than I ever thought I could. And that's why I'm asking again. Shine your light into his heart. Help him to see the truth of your ways and come to follow you—so that he will be not only my husband and king, but my Christian brother. This I pray in Jesus' name. Amen."

Malcolm turned to his advisor, not certain whether to shout for anger or for joy.

"She's praying, you fool! That's what she's doing in this cave. She's not with another man. She's praying to her God!" And then the king added, more quietly: "She's praying for me."

Queen Margaret turned around, startled by the voices.

"Who's there?" she called.

And the king had no choice but to answer. "It's me," he said softly. "It's your husband, the king."

Then he threw himself at her feet. "Forgive me," he begged. "I doubted you and, all the time, you were only showing your concern for me."

But when he told her what had happened, she just smiled and stroked his head.

"You followed me to this cave because you love me. And it was my love for you that brought me here in the first place. There is nothing to forgive in that."

And so they went home, king and queen, through forest, fern, and fog. And it wasn't long before Margaret's prayers were answered—and the king of Scotland bowed his knee before the King of Kings.

*M*argaret never forgot the Forest of Dunfermline. She built a church there, in fact, in celebration of her marriage. She dedicated it to the Trinity and to her most important goals in life: the salvation of her husband, her children, and herself.

She was only thirty-eight when she died, worn out by a life of devoted service to her family and her nation. So she did not live to see how thoroughly several of her goals came true. Two of her sons became monks, and three others—Edgar, Alexander, and David—became some of the best kings Scotland ever had. Her daughter, Matilda, married Henry I, king of England; and, following the example of her mother, ruled with such kindness and justice that she was forever after known as Good Queen Maud.

Talk about It

- Have you ever prayed for something over and over again—perhaps that a sick friend or relative might get better, or that some bad situation might be fixed? Talk about how that made you feel, particularly when you didn't get an answer from God right away.

- There is probably someone you know—a friend, a relative, a workmate—who does not follow Jesus. Start to pray for that person, just like Margaret prayed for Malcolm. Do it regularly every day, every week, whatever suits you. Then watch and see what happens.

Prayer

Dear God,
The world is full of people who do not yet know your love, who have not received your forgiveness, and who do not have the hope of your eternal life. Some of those people are in our families, our schools, our places of work; and we struggle, like Queen Margaret did, to know how best to tell them about you. Teach us what to say. Show us what to do. And use us, like you used Margaret, to draw the ones we love to you. Amen.

Salt and Pepper

SAINT HUGH OF LINCOLN
A.D. 1135–1200

What do you think of when you hear the word "pepper"? Something hot and burning? A strong spice that's not to everyone's taste?

When Hugh of Lincoln was asked to describe himself, the word he used was "peppery." Strong-willed, hot-tempered, intolerant of evil—that was Hugh, a monk who defended common people and who left a bad taste in the mouth of more than one English king.

King Henry II appointed Hugh bishop of Lincoln—a very important position—in eastern England. Bishops were known to bend to wishes of the kings who appointed them. Did this make Hugh easier to control? Not for a minute! When Henry's heir to the throne, Richard the Lion-hearted, wanted money from the church to finance his wars, Bishop Hugh delivered his answer personally: NO! Richard was angry, but there was something about Hugh—his bravery, his determination—that Richard admired as well. And the two remained good friends.

But kings weren't the only ones who got a taste of Hugh's courage and intolerance of injustice. There was a time when he had to face an angry mob as well—made up of the common people he had so often defended. And he needed every last ounce of that "pepper" to see that justice was done.

"AWAY WITH THE JEWS! Away with the Jews!" The shouting echoed up and down the streets of Lincoln, through the markets and the shops, right to the top of the hill where Bishop Hugh waited in the cathedral.

"You know where that mob is coming, don't you?" asked an anxious priest named Martin. "It's coming here!"

"I know," the bishop nodded calmly, "I have seen it before. The townspeople borrow from the Jewish moneylenders. They sign a note promising they will pay the money back. The moneylenders leave the notes in a church or a cathedral for safekeeping. And when the townspeople cannot pay—or *will* not—they break into the church and destroy the notes."

"Well then, what shall we do?" asked another, even more anxious priest, named Philip. "Hide? Run away? Or just give them the notes?"

"We'll do none of those things," said Hugh firmly as he walked slowly to the entrance of the cathedral. "When evil comes knocking at your door, there is no choice—you must face it and stop it where it stands!"

Martin and Philip looked at each other and trembled. "Why, oh why," they wondered, "had they been called to serve under Bishop Hugh? He was the most famous of England's bishops by far. And the most powerful, too—responsible for more churches than anyone else. He was even a personal friend of the king. But why, oh why, did he have to be so stubborn?"

The crowd was getting closer now—almost to the top of the hill. The bishop and his priests could hear them shouting and swearing and banging their staffs against the ground. They could hear cries for help as well—the screams of those unfortunate moneylenders whom the mob had captured and beaten.

"They might beat us, too," whispered Martin to Philip.

"Of course they will," Philip whispered in return, "if they don't get what they want."

Bishop Hugh turned around and looked at his anxious priests.

"If you wish to hide," he sighed, "I won't stand in your way."

And so, to a chorus of "Thank you" and "Thank you very much," Martin and Philip and all the other priests scattered throughout the cathedral, ducking behind altar and font and pews.

"Episcopi semper pavidi," the bishop muttered to himself. "Bishops are always timid." It was a popular saying. And, yes, it did apply to most of the bishops he knew—and to many priests as well, if his lot were anything to go by. But it most certainly did not apply to him!

Bishop Hugh grinned. Meekness was a Christian virtue. He understood that. But defending the weak and the poor and the stranger—was that not a virtue as well? And so, sometimes, it was necessary for bishops not only to kneel and pray, but to stand and fight, to face knights and noblemen and even kings in order to protect those who had no other protection.

Hugh had faced them all, and more often than not, he had come away victorious. But a violent mob was banging on the cathedral door now, and Hugh couldn't help wondering if he would be as successful with them.

The bishop offered up a quick prayer for courage and for wisdom. Then he threw open the cathedral doors.

Hundreds of townspeople stood before him, their faces red and angry, their voices full of hate.

"Away with the Jews!" they shouted. "Away with the Jews!"

Slowly, steadily, firmly, Bishop Hugh raised his right hand. He did not blink. He did not move. He did not speak. And when the crowd grew tired of waiting and finally settled down, he said, as calmly and as quietly as he could: "Go home. There are no Jews here."

"We know that!" called out one of the mob's leaders. "But their notes are here—the papers that say what each of us owes. We want them. And we want them now!"

"Those papers are here for safekeeping," Hugh explained. "As are the papers and deeds that belong to so many of you. The cathedral is a place of protection, a place of sanctuary."

"Not for Jews!" shouted someone else.

"For everyone!" the bishop shouted back. "For all men and women. Jews do not believe what we do. But they are no less human than we. God made them, too, and loves them as he loves us!"

"But they crucified his Son!" shouted another voice. "You should know that better than any of us!"

"NO! NO!" the bishop insisted. "These Jews have done nothing wrong. They are as innocent as our Savior—a Jew himself—whom an angry mob beat and put to death. And the truth is that God's Son died for the sins of *all* people—including your sins and mine. You cannot blame the Jews for that.

"I will not have you excusing your bigotry and your greed with the sacrifice of our Lord," Bishop Hugh continued. "And I will not surrender the notes!"

"Then we shall take the notes by force!" shouted several voices at once.

The rest of the crowd cheered their approval and moved toward the door. But Hugh stood fast. He did not move. He did not back away.

"Very well then!" he shouted, as loudly as he could. "I declare that from this moment on, the cathedral will no longer be a place of protection. And so, Robert Baker," he called to one of the mob, "when the sheriff comes for you because you have been unjustly accused of theft, you will no longer have a place to hide. And so, James Miller," he called to another in the crowd, "when the forester comes after you to hang you by the neck because you poached the odd rabbit to feed your family, there will no longer be anyone here to defend you, either!"

The crowd grew suddenly quiet.

"Answer me," the bishop demanded, "is this cathedral to remain a place of refuge and safety or not? If I give in to the violence of this mob, then I shall be obliged to give in to the violence of sheriffs and kings, as well."

"But that's different," someone called. "We're just poor folk and sometimes we need protecting from the sheriff and his like. They steal from us and whip us and knock us about."

"And have you treated these poor Jews any differently?" the bishop asked. "The power of mace and sword. The power of fist and staff. It's all the same to the one who is beaten."

The townspeople looked at one another. The bishop was right, and they knew it. So, one by one, they lowered their heads and then their staffs, and walked quietly home.

When they had gone, however, the cathedral courtyard was still not empty. There were bodies on the ground, some of them barely alive—the Jewish moneylenders whom the crowd had beaten.

Bishop Hugh walked over to the closest man. He knelt down and cradled the man's swollen head in his arm.

"What shall we do?" came a voice from behind him. "What shall we do now?" It was Martin and Philip and the other priests.

"Fetch water," the bishop ordered, "and bandages. As many as you can find." Then he glanced down at the man who lay trembling and bloody in his arm. "The time for fighting is over," he sighed. "Now it's time to heal."

Lincoln Cathedral is one of the most beautiful and striking cathedrals in England. It sits like a crown, high on a hill in the middle of the town—a lighthouse of love and faith that can be seen all across the countryside. And it was Bishop Hugh who began the rebuilding of that cathedral, which resulted in the magnificent place of worship that stands to this day.

Jesus once said that Christians are like lighthouses, too: "You are the light of the world. A city set on a hill cannot be hid" (Matthew 5:14). It was his hope that, in a world darkened by sin and evil, his followers would shine as examples of God's goodness and love and mercy. It's fitting, then, that the cathedral which stands like a beacon above the city of Lincoln should have been built by a bishop whose life was also a lighthouse.

Jesus used another picture to describe his followers. He said that Christians should be salt. Salt is a preservative that keeps meat from spoiling. And, once again, Hugh fit the picture perfectly. By opposing the oppression of the king and the anti-Semitism of the crowd, he helped preserve his world from the rotting violence of injustice and hate.

But salt is not only a preservative. It's also a seasoning—like pepper! Salt and pepper—the perfect combination and the perfect description of Hugh—stubborn and merciful, courageous and kind, bishop and builder and saint.

Talk about It

- Is it ever right to be angry? Are there things worth getting angry about? In one of his New Testament letters, the apostle Paul said that Christians should "be angry, but do not sin." What do that saying and the example of Bishop Hugh have to teach us about the way we deal with our anger?

- The hatred of Jews that Hugh battled in Lincoln did not disappear with that small victory. It has persisted throughout the history of the Western world and, unfortunately, exists today. One of its most tragic results was what we call the Holocaust—the slaughter of six million Jews by the Nazis during the Second World War. What do you think causes such hatred? What can we do to make that kind of hatred go away? And what can we do to make sure such awful persecution never happens again?

Prayer

Dear God,
Sometimes the weak get stepped on by the strong. Sometimes the poor are taken advantage of by the rich. Sometimes those who are different are treated like they are hardly human at all. In those times, O God, remind us of Hugh and give us the courage and compassion to act like he did—

    To defend the weak,
    To help the poor,
    And to welcome as friends those who are different from us.
Amen.

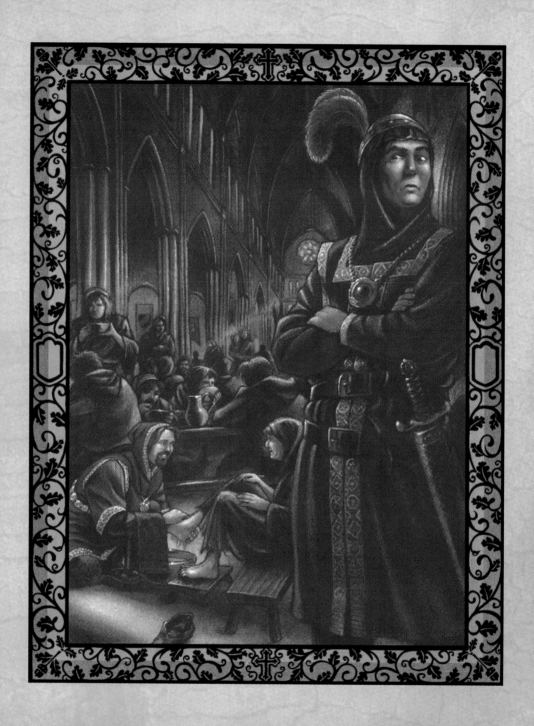

The Servant King

SAINT LOUIS
A.D. 1214–1270

nights in shining armor. Tournaments and jousts. High-walled, stone-faced castles. To you and me, these are the stuff of story and legend. But to twelve-year-old Louis, they were as common as ice cream and shopping malls are to us. What is more, when Louis's father died in 1226, the knights and tournaments and castles suddenly became his responsibility, for Louis was now King Louis IX of France!

Becoming king at the age of twelve might have spoiled some boys, but not Louis. His mother, Queen Blanche, ruled in his place for the next nine years, and she used that time to teach him how to be both a good Christian and a good king. So when Louis took the throne in 1235, he was ready to lead his people with compassion, justice, and wisdom.

Louis prayed regularly, forbade swearing in his presence, and worked hard to make peace among his quarreling noblemen. Like any king, Louis was rich, but he used the wealth to build hospitals and churches and to feed the poor.

The story of Louis's life was written shortly after his death by Jean of Joinville (zhahn of zhwahn-VEEL), his friend and secretary. Jean's biography of Louis is so interesting and full of love for the king that I decided to let him tell you the following story as well.

WHEN MY LORD, King Louis IX, made peace with the English king, an unending stream of princes, dukes, and noblemen made their way across the English Channel to visit us here in France.

Some were pleasant and easy-going. Some were stiff and formal. Most were, at the very least, polite. But the young duke who visited last year, on the Thursday before Easter, was simply annoying!

"Where is the king?" he demanded as he stripped off his riding gloves and slapped them into his hand. "I want to see the king!"

"All in good time," I assured him. "My name is Jean. Jean of Joinville. I am the king's secretary, responsible for his appointments and arrangements. He cannot see you at present, so he asked me to take you to the dining hall, where he will join you for supper."

I escorted him to the hall, and I could hear him behind me, fussing and huffing and muttering to himself.

"Stuck with some secretary!" he groused.

"And me," he bragged, "second cousin to the king of England himself!"

Then, without taking a breath, he started in again with the same questions.

"Where is the king?" he asked. "Does he even know I am here? Do you have any idea how important I am? I want to see the king!"

"Patience, sir," I said, growing impatient, myself. "The king is involved in some very important business. Please have something to eat while you wait."

He sat down at last, but the moment he looked at the table, the shouting began again.

"A knife!" he demanded. "And a glass of wine. And…what's this! No meat?"

"It is the Thursday before Easter," I reminded him. "Maundy Thursday, when we eat no meat in respect of our Savior."

"Yes, yes," he grumbled. "I'd quite forgotten that, what with the journey and all. I shall have to content myself with bread and fruit."

"Flute?" interrupted an old and quivering voice. "Did you say you play the flute?"

The voice belonged to William of Artois (ar-TWAH), an ancient knight who was seated next to the young duke, and whose hearing had been damaged in the wars to recapture Jerusalem from the Turkish Muslims.

"Not flute," I explained. "Fruit. The young gentleman will be eating fruit."

"WHILE I WAIT TO SEE THE KING!" the duke shouted in old William's ear.

"Ahhh, the king!" William smiled. "A good man—loyal and honest, kind and brave. The best knight I have ever known."

Then his eyes glazed over, and I knew a story was bound to follow.

"I can see him now," the old knight continued. "On that morning in Egypt, when we took the town of Mansura (man-SUR-uh). The enemy was all around. Many of us had fallen. But there he was, astride his horse in the thick of the battle, his armor bright as the burning sun!

"Six soldiers—six, mind you!—threw themselves at him. But he fought them off, each and every one, and led us to victory that day!"

"Let me tell you more of the king's bravery," added Lord Raymond of Champagne, who sat opposite the duke.

"On our return from Egypt, our ship struck a sandbar off the coast of Cyprus and was badly damaged. All of us—that is, those noblemen whom His Majesty consulted—encouraged him to see to his own safety, and to leave the damaged ship and board one of the others in our fleet.

"But the king said, 'No. I will not leave. There are five hundred people on this ship, many of them poor. If I abandon it they will not have confidence to stay aboard. And then their only chance will be to remain here in Cyprus. Who knows how long it will be till they can afford to return to France? No. We shall remain on the ship—all of us. And trust the Lord together.'"

The Englishman was applauding now. "Take me to him! Do it at once! I can wait no longer to meet such a brave and noble man. Take me to the king!"

I looked carefully around the hall till I saw what I needed to see.

"The king is not quite finished . . ." I began, and as the duke raised his finger to interrupt, I continued, "but I think it may be helpful for you to see him now. Come with me."

I walked as slowly as he would let me—past tables filled with counts and dukes and knights. Some of the noblest men in all France. But then the company changed.

"What is that smell?" the Englishman sniffed. "And who are these people?"

"Beggars. Widows. The poor and the sick." I answered.

"And what are they doing here?" he demanded to know.

"Eating."

"Yes, I can see that. But why here? Do they not have homes of their own? Must they come and pollute such noble company?"

"Sir!" I said, quickly turning around to face him, "these *are* noble company, just like yourself—guests, whom the king has invited to his table."

"At . . . Eastertime?" the duke stammered.

"All the time," I replied. "But there are perhaps a few more because of the season."

"But how can he stand it?" the duke asked. "They smell so foul, and—look at them—their clothes, their hair; they're so dirty!"

"Not at all," I assured him. "Look closely. Their hands and faces are clean. And here, here is someone washing their feet!"

The duke looked down at a man with a towel, bent over the gnarled toes of an old peasant. Then he turned away in disgust.

"I have waited long enough!" the Englishman fumed. "You told me we were going to see the king, and instead you surround me with beggars. Where is the king? I want to see the king!"

The man with the towel stood up and turned around.

"And so you shall," he said.

The duke looked at the man's face. Then at his clothes. And finally at the pendant that hung from a gold chain around his neck.

"Y-your Majesty," he stuttered. "I . . . didn't . . . know."

"I can see that," said the king softly. "But do you understand? That is the important thing."

The Englishman looked at me—for an answer, I suppose. Then he looked back at the king and sadly shook his head. "Not at all," he said. "Not at all."

And so King Louis explained. "Many years ago, on the Thursday before that very first Easter, the King of Heaven ate a special meal with his followers. And at that meal, he himself knelt down and washed the feet of poor and humble fishermen and their friends. Compared to him, I am a poor excuse for a king, but I count it a great honor to kneel down once a year and follow his example."

"I see," muttered the duke. "Well, it has been a great honor to meet you. But I can see that you are busy. And I will now wait at my table until you are finished."

"Nonsense," said the king. "You came all this way to see me. You are a valued guest. Why not join me? Here. Now."

The Englishman smiled at first, and then, I believe, the full meaning of the king's invitation dawned on him. And his smile gave way to an expression that more closely resembled shock.

"Y-you don't mean," he stammered, "that I should kneel down among these beggars and . . . and . . ."

"Jean," the king said to me with a wink, "bring the duke a towel!"

*L*ouis IX may have been a successful king and a faithful follower of the Lord, but he was a hopeless Crusader. For 150 years, Christian kings had been leading armies into the Middle East to win Jerusalem back from Turkish Muslims. To join these Crusades (as the attempts were called) was considered an act of great faith. Unfortunately, they often turned into bloody excuses for destruction and murder on the part of the invading armies. Many historians consider the Crusades cruel disasters, and they were certainly disastrous for Louis. During the Seventh Crusade (1248–1254) the king of France was captured and had to pay a huge ransom to be released. And in the Eighth Crusade (1270), Louis caught typhoid fever and died.

Within thirty years of his death, the church declared Louis a saint for his life of humility and service to God. And what is more, if you look closely at a map of the United States, you will find a famous city on the Mississippi River that was named after him.

Talk about It

- In this story, the duke thought he was better than some people Louis had invited to his table—poor, sick, homeless people. He didn't want to be around those people, didn't even want to look at them. Do you know anyone who feels this way about poor, sick, and homeless people today? What causes such feelings?

- Are there people whom *you* would rather not be around? People whom you would rather not have as friends? Why do we sometimes feel we are better than others? And what could you do to change those feelings in yourself?

Prayer

Dear God,
Sometimes we think we are better than other people. Forgive us when that kind of prejudice enters our hearts. Sometimes we would rather not be around—or even think about—those who are poor or sick or needy. Open our eyes and our hearts to anyone we meet. Help us treat everyone with love, help us do whatever we can for those in need—even if that means stooping to wash and dry a pair of dirty feet. Amen.

Wonder Bread

SAINT ZITA
A.D. 1218–1278

aving cities. Founding towns. Facing mobs. Preserving civilization. Many of the saints we have met so far have accomplished great things. But Zita's work took place on a much smaller scale. From the time she was twelve, Zita (ZEE-tuh) was a simple servant in the household of Signor Fatinelli (seen-YOR Fat-i-NELL-ee), a weaver who lived in the Italian town of Lucca.

She never stood up to a king or challenged an army or miraculously saved someone's life. Hers was an everyday kind of goodness that is perhaps the best example for the kinds of lives we are likely to lead. Her everyday life was marked by kindness, faithfulness, patience, and sacrifice—not just once in a while, but day by day, quietly, and without recognition or reward. Maybe that steady, quiet goodness really is the greatest accomplishment of all—a wonder that God chose to reward with a wonder all his own!

"Zita! Run the water."

"Zita! Fetch the wood."

"Zita! Sweep the stairs."

"Zita! Wash the clothes."

The orders never seemed to stop. And neither did Zita! Like a real-life Cinderella, she worked hard from morning to night. She worked with care and pride. She worked without grumbling. And her fellow servants did not like that one bit.

"Zita makes us look bad."

"Zita works far too much."

"Zita thinks she's better than us."

The whispering never seemed to stop. But Zita tried hard to ignore it. She worked even harder, and went to church each day to pray and to ask for God's help.

One morning while it was still quite dark, she wrapped a shawl around her and picked her way through the silent house. She stooped to pet the cat. She checked on her master's children. Then she finished up in the kitchen, where she laid out spoons and bowls and flour—ready for the bread she would bake on her return.

When all was prepared, she slipped quietly out the back door and down the stony streets of Lucca.

This was her favorite time of the day. It wasn't just the absence of her master's angry voice or her fellow servants' jealous whispers. It was the pink-grey light, the waking cry of the doves, and the way the sleepy town shook itself, citizen by citizen, out of its long night slumber. A child at a window. A servant opening a door. The first trader at the market. Zita noticed them all. But her focus was on the church in the center of town where she and a few others gathered each morning to pray.

Zita prayed for her master, Signor Fatinelli, and for his wife and children. She prayed for the other servants—the butler, the lady-in-waiting, the maids. But all the while, she was troubled. Her master took advantage of her—she knew that—and gave her more work than the others simply because she always did it without complaint. But still he shouted at her and lost his temper, just as he did with the butler or the maids. As for them, even though she often took on work they were supposed to do, they were never the least bit grateful.

Maybe the other servants were right. Maybe she was a fool to do so much for so little reward. Working hard. Helping out. Serving the master as if he were God himself. That, she knew, was the right thing to do. But why was it so hard? And why did everyone seem to dislike her for it? Zita put her head in her hands as she silently shared each and every worry with God.

Finally, she prayed: "Dear God, Show me. Show me if I am still on the right path—the path you have set for me."

Zita rose and slowly walked out of the church. But as soon as she stepped outside the tall doors, she knew something was wrong! The streets were much busier than usual, the market more crowded, the sun much higher in the sky.

"Hello, Zita!" called a neighbor's maid. "You're out late this morning! Don't tell me old Fatinelli has finally given you a day off?"

Zita nodded and smiled politely at the joke. But she knew inside that there was nothing funny about this situation. She'd spent too much time over her prayers, and now she was late. Now she was in trouble. And . . . the bread. The bread! She'd forgotten completely about the bread!

Her thoughts were racing now—darting, panicked, flashing through her head. And it was all her feet could do to keep up with them, for each stony step brought with it a new fear.

The master will shout!

The master will swear!

The master will strike me and cast me out into the street!

The house was not far from the church, but it could have been miles away as far as Zita was concerned. She was already late, already in trouble. No wonder it seemed an eternity before she at last ducked into the back door.

She was puffing hard at first—catching her breath. And perhaps that is why she did not notice it. But as soon as she settled down, she smelled it—floating out of the kitchen and down the hall to greet her: the crusty aroma of fresh-baked bread!

"This is not possible," she thought. But when she stuck her head into the kitchen, there they were—two huge, fresh, brown loaves!

"But who could have baked them?" Zita wondered. The kitchen was empty, the tools undisturbed, and even though she looked, Zita found no note, no explanation.

Confusion, that's what Zita felt. And then, suddenly, her confusion turned into a kind of surprised joy.

"Of course!" Zita thought. "Someone in this house has come around at last. They saw the trouble I was in, and just like I have done so many times for them, they covered for me! It was one of the other servants who baked the bread. But which one?"

Zita threw off her shawl and hurried up the stairs. The maids were busy making the beds—and gossiping to one another.

"Excuse me . . . ," Zita interrupted.

But before she could ask her very important question, one of the maids burst out: "Oh, Zita! There you are. I know I've never said it before, but you bake the best bread in all of Lucca. And the smell today . . . Well, all I can say is that I can't wait until lunch!"

"But that's what I was going to ask," Zita protested. "You see, I can't really take responsibility for that bread."

"Oh, Zita!" the second maid giggled. "You're too modest. Far too modest. Do you think you could save an extra-big slice for me?"

"Yes. Certainly. Of course," muttered Zita as she stumbled out of the bedroom, anxious to find the other servants.

She talked with the butler next, and then the lady-in-waiting. She even had a word with the stable boy. But each of them assumed Zita had baked the bread and praised her like she had never been praised before.

Now Zita was more confused than ever.

"Who could have done it?" she wondered. "If not a servant, then . . . ? No, never! It could not possibly be!"

But Zita had to be sure. So she knocked as politely as she could on the door of Signor Fatinelli.

"Zita!" he shouted when he had opened the door. But it was not his usual angry shout. No, it was the shout of a man who has just spotted a long-lost friend.

"Zita!" he shouted again. And he threw his arms around her! "Zita, I have been waiting all morning to congratulate you. You are a good servant. The best I have! And I admit it—yes I do—I have taken you for granted. But this time, you have outdone yourself! That bread . . . That bread . . .

"There is no other word for it. The smell of that bread is . . . *heavenly!*"

And that's when Zita knew. Standing there in front of her master, Zita's confusion turned once again into surprise and joy. That bread had not been made by anyone in the house—not by master, nor butler, nor maid. No, that bread had come from heaven, baked by the hands of an angel in answer to her prayers!

Zita thanked her master for his compliments. Then she hurried back to the kitchen and fell to her knees, where she gave thanks to her Heavenly Master as well.

And from that moment on, everything changed for Zita. Signor Fatinelli took more notice of her hard work. And when the other servants angered him, it was Zita—and Zita alone—who could calm the master and ease his wrath. So, eventually, their jealousy gave way to a deep respect for Zita, and they came to recognize the sweet smell of heaven, not only in her bread, but in the way she lived her life.

*Z*ita *worked in the Fatinelli household for the rest of her life. And as the years passed, she was not only given more responsibility but also more freedom. Did she use that freedom for herself? Not Zita. No, she gave to the poor and helped the sick and visited the prisoners in jail. And the kindness of this simple household servant, as well as her love for God, spread all across the town.*

Talk about It

- In the New Testament book of Mark, chapter 10, verses 35-45, Jesus talks with his followers about the nature of "greatness." He tells them that the greatest person is not the one with the most power, but the one who is the best servant. Who are some people you know who are great because of the way they care for others? What are some ways to thank them for their kindness?

- Sometimes it's the little, daily acts of kindness that make the biggest differences in our lives. What little, kind thing could you do for someone in your family, church, or neighborhood that would make a big difference in that person's life? Don't just talk about it. Follow Zita's example and do it!

Prayer

Dear God,

You have shown us that greatness comes with service, and that little acts of kindness make a big difference in the lives of those around us. Keep our eyes open and our ears sharp that we may recognize the needs of others. And fill us with the compassion to help and the humility to act—even if no one else ever knows what we have done. Amen.